most loved recipe collection most loved recipe collection

most loved

loved

casseroles

Pictured on front cover:
Easy Shepherd's Pie, page 25

Pictured on back cover:
Mediterranean Chicken And Bean Casserole, page 44

Most Loved Casseroles

Copyright © Company's Coming Publishing Limited

First Printing November 2006

Library and Archives Canada Cataloguing in Publication
Paré, Jean, date
Most loved casseroles / by Jean Paré.
(Most loved recipe collection)
Includes index.
ISBN 1-897069-07-3
1. Casserole cookery. I. Title. II. Series: Paré, Jean, date. Most loved recipe collection.
TX693.P375 2006   641.8'21   C2006-901956-8

Published by
Company's Coming Publishing Limited
2311 – 96 Street
Edmonton, Alberta, Canada T6N 1G3
Tel: 780-450-6223   Fax: 780-450-1857
www.companyscoming.com

Company's Coming is a registered trademark owned by
Company's Coming Publishing Limited

Printed in China

We gratefully acknowledge the following suppliers for their generous support of our Test and Photography Kitchens:

Broil King Barbecue®
Corelle®
Hamilton Beach® Canada
Lagostina®
Proctor Silex® Canada
Tupperware®

Our special thanks to the following businesses for providing props for photography:

Anchor Hocking Canada
Canhome Global
Casa Bugatti
Cherison Enterprises Inc.
Chintz & Company
Corningware®
Danesco Inc.
Dansk Gifts
Emile Henry
Island Pottery Inc.
Linens 'N Things
Mikasa Home Store
Out of the Fire Studio
Pfaltzgraff Canada
Pier 1 Imports
Stokes
The Basket House
The Bay
The Dazzling Gourmet
Totally Bamboo
Wiltshire®
Winners Stores

Pictured from left: Ham And Pasta Bake, page 114; Pork And Rice Dish, page 103; Biscuit-Topped Casserole, page 22; Hamburger Pacific, page 8

table of contents

"never share a recipe you wouldn't use yourself"

the Company's Coming story

Jean Paré (pronounced "jeen PAIR-ee") grew up understanding that the combination of family, friends and home cooking is the best recipe for a good life. From her mother, she learned to appreciate good cooking, while her father praised even her earliest attempts in the kitchen. When Jean left home, she took with her a love of cooking, many family recipes and an intriguing desire to read cookbooks as if they were novels!

In 1963, when her four children had all reached school age, Jean volunteered to cater the 50th Anniversary of the Vermilion School of Agriculture, now Lakeland College, in Alberta, Canada. Working out of her home, Jean prepared a dinner for more than 1,000 people, which launched a flourishing catering operation that continued for over 18 years. During that time, she had countless opportunities to test new ideas with immediate feedback—resulting in empty plates and contented customers! Whether preparing cocktail sandwiches for a house party or serving a hot meal for 1,500 people, Jean Paré earned a reputation for good food, courteous service and reasonable prices.

As requests for her recipes mounted, Jean was often asked the question, "Why don't you write a cookbook?" Jean responded by teaming up with her son, Grant Lovig, in the fall of 1980 to form Company's Coming Publishing Limited. The publication of *150 Delicious Squares* on April 14, 1981 marked the debut of what would soon become one of the world's most popular cookbook series.

The company has grown since those early days when Jean worked from a spare bedroom in her home. Today, she continues to write recipes while working closely with the staff of the Recipe Factory, as the Company's Coming test kitchen is affectionately known. There she fills the role of mentor, assisting with the development of recipes people most want to use for everyday cooking and easy entertaining. Every Company's Coming recipe is *kitchen-tested* before it's approved for publication.

Jean's daughter, Gail Lovig, is responsible for marketing and distribution, leading a team that includes sales personnel located in major cities across Canada. In addition, Company's Coming cookbooks are published and distributed under licence in the United States, Australia and other world markets. Bestsellers many times over in English, Company's Coming cookbooks have also been published in French and Spanish.

Familiar and trusted in home kitchens around the world, Company's Coming cookbooks are offered in a variety of formats. Highly regarded as kitchen workbooks, the softcover Original Series, with its lay-flat plastic comb binding, is still a favourite among readers.

Jean Paré's approach to cooking has always called for *quick and easy recipes* using *everyday ingredients*. That view has served her well. The recipient of many awards, including the Queen Elizabeth Golden Jubilee medal, Jean was appointed a Member of the Order of Canada, her country's highest lifetime achievement honour.

Jean continues to gain new supporters by adhering to what she calls The Golden Rule of Cooking: *"Never share a recipe you wouldn't use yourself."* It's an approach that works— *millions of times over!*

foreword

No one knows who invented the first casserole. But it's easy to imagine some long-ago housewife, bogged down with milking the goats or scrubbing her laundry at the local stream, trying to come up with an easy and convenient supper. Did she just toss all the ingredients into one pot, cover it, put it over the fire and hope for the best? It was inspiration at its best, and busy, modern-day families are forever grateful.

A casserole is more than just a delicious one-dish meal that cuts down on the dishwashing at the end of the day. It's the favourite family recipe handed down like a treasured heirloom, the welcome gift after the baby is born, and the pot of gold at the back of the freezer when you're fresh out of dinner ideas. Pop one into the oven and let it bubble along as the flavours mingle, the textures grow tender and the aroma wafts through the house, welcoming every newcomer with the promise of a delicious meal. It's comfort food at its best.

With its combination of vegetables, protein and starches, a casserole is also the ultimate make-ahead meal. Cook up a double batch and freeze the extra dish. Let it thaw overnight in the fridge and the next day a well-balanced dinner is ready to go into the oven. Or divide the casserole into individual servings and freeze for handy lunches.

The word casserole has two meanings. There's the actual vessel, traditionally an earthenware pot with a lid—nowadays a piece of foil will turn almost any oven-proof container into a casserole dish, allowing you to experiment with everything from pie plates to roasting pans. Casserole also refers to the food cooked in the dish. It first appeared in an English cookbook in 1708, describing a rice crust filled with chicken or sweetbreads. Eventually, any one-dish, oven-cooked meal came to be known as a casserole, even though its recipe title might call it a pie or a bake or even a lasagna. That's why you'll find everything from moussaka and strata to shepherd's pie in *Most Loved Casseroles*.

You'll also find handy tips, fun food facts and interesting background information about a recipe's history or ingredients. From a brief primer on asparagus and an explanation of jambalaya to a history of Worcestershire sauce, it's all here. With this wonderful collection of *Most Loved Casseroles*, you'll soon find your own favourites to add to your family's traditions.

Jean Paré

nutrition information

Each recipe is analyzed using the most current version of the Canadian Nutrient File from Health Canada, which is based on the United States Department of Agriculture (USDA) Nutrient Database.

- If more than one ingredient is listed (such as "hard margarine or butter"), or if a range is given (1 – 2 tsp., 5 – 10 mL), only the first ingredient or first amount is analyzed.

- For meat, poultry and fish, the serving size per person is based on the recommended 4 oz. (113 g) uncooked weight (without bone), which is 2 – 3 oz. (57 – 85 g) cooked weight (without bone)—approximately the size of a deck of playing cards.

- Milk used is 1% M.F. (milk fat), unless otherwise stated.

- Cooking oil used is canola oil, unless otherwise stated.

- Ingredients indicating "sprinkle," "optional," or "for garnish" are not included in the nutrition information.

Margaret Ng, B.Sc. (Hon.), M.A.
Registered Dietitian

*A casserole with Mexican flair!
Serve with a spinach salad for a
complete meal.*

baking dish sizes

Baking dishes come in many
sizes, so you must always be
aware of the nasty consequences
of choosing a wrong-sized dish!
If your dish is too large, too much
moisture will evaporate, leaving
you with a somewhat dehydrated
dinner. If your dish is too small,
much of the mixture will bubble
up and make a mess of your oven.
If your dish is too shallow, you
may burn or overcook your food.
If your dish is too deep, your food
may be undercooked. If you're not
sure what size your baking dishes
are, just fill them with water and
measure the amount you pour
out. The amount of water a dish
holds is its volume. It is also
important to note that a casserole
dish has higher sides than a
regular baking dish—meaning a
shallow baking dish of the same
volume cannot be substituted for
a casserole dish. So, avoid kitchen
catastrophes by always using the
correct size and type of dish
suggested in each recipe.

Zesty Beef Casserole

Cooking oil	1 tsp.	5 mL
Lean ground beef	1 lb.	454 g
Chopped onion	1 cup	250 mL
Chopped green pepper	1/2 cup	125 mL
Chopped red pepper	1/2 cup	125 mL
Can of stewed tomatoes (with juice), chopped	14 oz.	398 mL
Medium egg noodles	2 cups	500 mL
Can of kernel corn (with liquid)	12 oz.	341 mL
Water	1 1/4 cups	300 mL
Can of diced green chilies	4 oz.	113 g
Envelope of taco seasoning mix	1 1/4 oz.	35 g
Salt	1/2 tsp.	2 mL
Pepper	1/4 tsp.	1 mL
Grated jalapeño Monterey Jack cheese	1 cup	250 mL

Sliced black olives, for garnish

Heat cooking oil in large frying pan on medium. Add next 4 ingredients.
Scramble-fry for about 10 minutes until beef is no longer pink. Drain.

Add tomatoes with juice. Stir. Transfer to ungreased 3 quart (3 L) casserole.

Add next 7 ingredients. Stir. Bake, covered, in 350°F (175°C) oven for about
1 hour, stirring once at halftime, until noodles are tender but firm.

Sprinkle with cheese. Bake, uncovered, for another 5 to 10 minutes until cheese
is melted.

Garnish with olives. Serves 6.

*1 serving: 349 Calories; 15.0 g Total Fat (5.5 g Mono, 1.2 g Poly, 6.7 g Sat); 68 mg Cholesterol;
33 g Carbohydrate; 4 g Fibre; 23 g Protein; 1217 mg Sodium*

Pictured at right.

With thin noodles and cream-style corn, this ground beef dish is different from others you've tried. You'll love its unique flavour!

variation

There are many varieties of stir-fry mixes on the market. Explore your options by using ones with ingredients you don't often cook with, such as bean sprouts, water chestnuts and sugar snap peas.

Hamburger Pacific

Cooking oil	1 tbsp.	15 mL
Lean ground beef	2 lbs.	900 g
Chopped onion	1 cup	250 mL
Garlic clove, minced (or 1/4 tsp., 1 mL, powder)	1	1
Salt	2 tsp.	10 mL
Pepper	1/2 tsp.	2 mL
Can of cream-style corn	14 oz.	398 mL
Can of sliced mushrooms, drained	10 oz.	284 mL
Can of condensed tomato soup	10 oz.	284 mL
Fresh (or frozen) stir-fry vegetable mix	2 cups	500 mL
Fresh Chinese thin egg noodles	7 oz.	200 g
Boiling water		
Paprika, sprinkle		

Heat cooking oil in large frying pan on medium. Add next 5 ingredients. Scramble-fry for about 10 minutes until beef is no longer pink. Drain.

Add next 3 ingredients. Stir. Transfer to greased 3 quart (3 L) casserole.

Scatter vegetables over beef mixture. Set aside.

Put noodles into medium heatproof bowl. Cover with boiling water. Stir. Let stand for about 1 minute until softened. Drain well. Layer on top of vegetables.

Sprinkle with paprika. Bake, covered, in 350°F (175°C) oven for 50 to 60 minutes until heated through. Serves 8.

1 serving: 372 Calories; 13.5 g Total Fat (5.8 g Mono, 1.6 g Poly, 4.3 g Sat); 81 mg Cholesterol; 38 g Carbohydrate; 3 g Fibre; 27 g Protein; 1157 mg Sodium

Pictured at right.

A great way to turn leftover macaroni into a delicious meal. Serve this simple version of pastitsio, a traditional layered Greek dish that is similar to lasagna, with a Greek salad.

multi-use baking dishes

Before spending your hard-earned dollars on a baking dish there are other things, besides size, that you should consider:

• Do you plan for your casserole to go right from the oven to the dining table? If so, you may want to invest in a more decorative vessel. There is an endless selection of stylish dishes to choose from. You can buy almost any colour, you can opt for painted designs, you can even buy dishes in the shapes of hearts and apples!

• Do you like to make recipes in advance and freeze them? If so, invest in a dish that is designed to go both in the oven and in the freezer. Many of these containers are sold with resealable lids.

Creamy Greek Bake

Light salad dressing (or mayonnaise)	1/2 cup	125 mL
All-purpose flour	1/4 cup	60 mL
Salt	1/2 tsp.	2 mL
Milk	2 cups	500 mL
Cooking oil	1 tsp.	5 mL
Lean ground beef	1 lb.	454 g
Chopped onion	1 cup	250 mL
Garlic clove, minced (or 1/4 tsp., 1 mL, powder)	1	1
Can of tomato paste	5 1/2 oz.	156 mL
Ground cinnamon	1/4 tsp.	1 mL
Cooked elbow macaroni (about 3/4 cup, 175 mL, uncooked)	1 1/2 cups	375 mL
Grated Parmesan cheese	1/2 cup	125 mL
Large egg, fork-beaten	1	1
Ground nutmeg	1/4 tsp.	1 mL
Paprika	1/8 tsp.	0.5 mL

Combine first 3 ingredients in medium saucepan.

Slowly add milk, stirring constantly until smooth. Heat and stir on medium for about 10 minutes until boiling and thickened. Transfer to medium heatproof bowl. Cover with plastic wrap directly on surface to prevent skin from forming. Set aside.

Heat cooking oil in large frying pan on medium. Add next 3 ingredients. Scramble-fry for about 10 minutes until beef is no longer pink. Drain.

Add tomato paste and cinnamon. Stir. Transfer to greased 2 quart (2 L) casserole.

Add next 4 ingredients to milk mixture. Stir. Spread over beef mixture.

Sprinkle with paprika. Bake, covered, in 350°F (175°C) oven for 40 minutes. Bake, uncovered, for another 10 to 15 minutes until set and golden. Serves 4.

1 serving: 570 Calories; 26.4 g Total Fat (11.7 g Mono, 3.7 g Poly, 8.3 g Sat); 126 mg Cholesterol; 46 g Carbohydrate; 4 g Fibre; 37 g Protein; 950 mg Sodium

Pictured on page 13.

Teener's Dish

Cooking oil	1 tsp.	5 mL
Lean ground beef	1 lb.	454 g
Chopped onion	1 cup	250 mL
Medium green pepper, cut into thin strips	1	1
Frozen kernel corn	1 1/2 cups	375 mL
Salt	3/4 tsp.	4 mL
Pepper	1/4 tsp.	1 mL
Fusilli (or other spiral) pasta	2 cups	500 mL
Tomato juice	3 cups	750 mL
Grated light sharp Cheddar cheese	1 cup	250 mL

Heat cooking oil in large frying pan on medium. Add next 3 ingredients. Scramble-fry for about 10 minutes until beef is no longer pink. Drain.

Add next 3 ingredients. Stir.

Put 1 cup (250 mL) of pasta into greased 3 quart (3 L) casserole. Spoon 1/2 of beef mixture onto pasta. Layer with remaining pasta and beef mixture.

Pour tomato juice over top. Bake, covered, in 350°F (175°C) oven for about 50 minutes until pasta is tender.

Sprinkle with cheese. Bake, uncovered, for another 5 to 10 minutes until cheese is melted. Serves 4.

1 serving: 602 Calories; 24 g Total Fat (9.6 g Mono, 1.8 g Poly, 9.8 g Sat); 77 mg Cholesterol; 62 g Carbohydrate; 5 g Fibre; 36 g Protein; 1361 mg Sodium

Give yourself a break and have your teens make supper tonight. They won't even have to precook the pasta—it can't get simpler than that!

variation

Are you feeling the need for a little variety? Shake things up by changing the cheese. If you like a little zip, substitute with a jalapeño Monterey Jack or Mexican blend. Not that adventurous yet? Use a different age of Cheddar. Just remember: the longer the cheese is aged, the sharper the taste.

Savoury onion flavour combines with pasta and veggies to make this ground beef casserole a real winner.

One-Dish Meal

Penne (or other tube) pasta	2 2/3 cups	650 mL
Cooking oil	1 tsp.	5 mL
Lean ground beef	1 lb.	454 g
All-purpose flour	2 tbsp.	30 mL
Cans of condensed onion soup (10 oz., 284 mL, each)	2	2
Water (1 soup can)	10 oz.	284 mL
Frozen peas and carrots	2 cups	500 mL
Can of sliced mushrooms, drained (or 2 cups, 500 mL, sliced fresh white mushrooms)	10 oz.	284 mL
French-fried onions	1/2 cup	125 mL

Cook pasta in boiling salted water in large uncovered saucepan or Dutch oven for 8 to 10 minutes, stirring occasionally, until tender but firm. Drain. Set aside.

Heat cooking oil in large frying pan on medium. Add beef. Scramble-fry for about 10 minutes until no longer pink. Drain.

Add flour. Heat and stir for 1 minute.

Add soup and water. Heat and stir for about 10 minutes until boiling and slightly thickened.

Add next 2 ingredients. Stir. Bring to a boil. Reduce heat to medium-low. Simmer, uncovered, for 2 minutes. Add to pasta. Stir. Transfer to ungreased 2 quart (2 L) casserole. Bake, covered, in 350°F (175°C) oven for 30 to 35 minutes until heated through.

Sprinkle with onions. Serves 6.

1 serving: 505 Calories; 21.7 g Total Fat (4.0 g Mono, 1.4 g Poly, 8.2 g Sat); 38 mg Cholesterol; 54 g Carbohydrate; 4 g Fibre; 24 g Protein; 1235 mg Sodium

Pictured at right.

Top left: One-Dish Meal, above
Bottom: Creamy Greek Bake, page 10

This delicious lasagna is extra meaty.
Serve with garlic toast.

Lasagna

MEAT SAUCE

Cooking oil	1 tbsp.	15 mL
Lean ground beef	2 lbs.	900 g
Chopped onion	1 1/4 cups	300 mL
Garlic clove, minced (or 1/4 tsp., 1 mL, powder)	1/4 tsp.	1 mL
Water	2 cups	500 mL
Can of tomato sauce	14 oz.	398 mL
Can of sliced mushrooms, drained	10 oz.	284 mL
Can of tomato paste	5 1/2 oz.	156 mL
Granulated sugar	1 tsp.	5 mL
Dried oregano	1/2 tsp.	2 mL
Salt	2 tsp.	10 mL
Pepper	1/4 tsp.	1 mL
Lasagna noodles	12	12
2% cottage cheese	2 cups	500 mL
Grated mozzarella cheese	4 cups	1 L
Grated Parmesan cheese	1/2 cup	125 mL

Meat Sauce: Heat cooking oil in large frying pan or Dutch oven on
medium-high. Add next 3 ingredients. Scramble-fry for about 10 minutes
until beef is no longer pink. Drain.

Add next 8 ingredients. Stir. Bring to a boil. Reduce heat to medium-low.
Simmer, uncovered, for 20 minutes, stirring occasionally. Makes about 7 cups
(1.75 L) sauce.

Cook noodles in boiling salted water in uncovered Dutch oven for 12 to
14 minutes, stirring occasionally, until tender but firm. Drain. Rinse with cold
water. Drain.

Layer ingredients in greased 9 x 13 inch (22 x 33 cm) pan as follows:
1. 1 cup (250 mL) meat sauce
2. 4 lasagna noodles
3. Cottage cheese
4. 2 cups (500 mL) mozzarella cheese

(continued on next page)

5. 2 cups (500 mL) meat sauce
6. 4 lasagna noodles
7. 2 cups (500 mL) meat sauce
8. 4 lasagna noodles
9. 2 cups (500 mL) meat sauce
10. 2 cups (500 mL) mozzarella cheese
11. Parmesan cheese

Bake, uncovered, in 350°F (175°C) oven for 45 to 55 minutes until heated through. Cover loosely with greased foil if cheese starts to brown too quickly. Let stand for 15 minutes before serving. Serves 8.

1 serving: 606 Calories; 28.5 g Total Fat (10.2 g Mono, 1.8 g Poly, 14.1 g Sat); 117 mg Cholesterol; 38 g Carbohydrate; 3 g Fibre; 49 g Protein; 1636 mg Sodium

Pictured below.

Almost as easy as ordering takeout—and just as tasty! You don't even need to precook the rice.

about water chestnuts

Don't be roasting your water chestnuts on an open fire! The water chestnut is not a nut at all but a bulb-like root that grows in water and marshes. The water chestnut is most prized for its ability to remain crisp and crunchy after cooking. It can be hard to get fresh water chestnuts in most countries so recipes often call for canned water chestnuts that can have a tinny taste. To get rid of this metallic flavour, briefly rinse with boiling water.

Chinese-Style Hash

Cooking oil	1 tsp.	5 mL
Lean ground beef	1 lb.	454 g
Chopped green pepper	1 1/2 cups	375 mL
Chopped onion	1 cup	250 mL
Chopped celery	1/2 cup	125 mL
Boiling water	1 cup	250 mL
Beef bouillon cubes (1/5 oz., 6 g, each)	3	3
Fresh bean sprouts	2 cups	500 mL
Can of sliced mushrooms, drained	10 oz.	284 mL
Can of sliced water chestnuts, drained	8 oz.	227 mL
Can of bamboo shoots, drained	8 oz.	227 mL
Long grain white rice	1/2 cup	125 mL
Soy sauce	3 tbsp.	50 mL
Salt	1 tsp.	5 mL
Pepper	1/4 tsp.	1 mL

Heat cooking oil in large frying pan on medium. Add beef. Scramble-fry for about 10 minutes until no longer pink. Drain.

Add next 3 ingredients. Cook for 5 to 10 minutes, stirring often, until onion is softened. Remove from heat.

Measure boiling water into small heatproof bowl. Add bouillon cubes. Stir until dissolved. Add to beef mixture. Stir.

Add remaining 8 ingredients. Stir. Transfer to ungreased 2 quart (2 L) casserole. Bake, covered, in 350°F (175°C) oven for about 45 minutes until rice is tender and liquid is absorbed. Serves 4.

1 serving: 382 Calories; 12.0 g Total Fat (5.2 g Mono, 1.0 g Poly, 4.2 g Sat); 57 mg Cholesterol; 41 g Carbohydrate; 5 g Fibre; 28 g Protein; 2374 mg Sodium

Pictured at right.

Top: Chinese-Style Hash, above
Bottom: Jambalaya Casserole, page 18

"Son of a gun, we'll have big fun on the bayou!" This recipe is quick and easy to put together, with fantastic results.

food fun

There is little consensus as to the origin of the name jambalaya but the most probable derivation is from the Spanish words *jamón* (ham) and *paella* (a Spanish dish that shares many of the same ingredients as jambalaya). Although the dish is thought to be specific to certain southern American states, there is certainly no adherence to one specific recipe. Often the variations differ in the meat used (beef, chicken, fish, shrimp, even alligator!) and the amount of heat added to the dish with ingredients like cayenne pepper and hot sauce.

Jambalaya Casserole

Cooking oil	1 tsp.	5 mL
Lean ground beef	1 lb.	454 g
Chopped onion	3/4 cup	175 mL
Garlic clove, minced (or 1/4 tsp., 1 mL, powder)	1	1
Can of stewed tomatoes (with juice), chopped	28 oz.	796 mL
Chopped green pepper	1 1/2 cups	375 mL
Long grain white rice	3/4 cup	175 mL
Chopped fresh parsley (or 3/4 tsp., 4 mL, flakes)	1 tbsp.	15 mL
Paprika	1 tsp.	5 mL
Worcestershire sauce	1/2 tsp.	2 mL
Chili powder	1/2 tsp.	2 mL
Bay leaf	1	1
Salt	1 tsp.	5 mL
Pepper	1/4 tsp.	1 mL

Heat cooking oil in large frying pan on medium. Add next 3 ingredients. Scramble-fry for about 10 minutes until beef is no longer pink. Drain. Transfer to greased 3 quart (3 L) casserole.

Add remaining 10 ingredients. Stir. Bake, covered, in 350°F (175°C) oven for about 1 1/4 hours until rice is tender and liquid is absorbed. Discard bay leaf. Serves 6.

1 serving: 271 Calories; 7.8 g Total Fat (3.4 g Mono, 0.7 g Poly, 2.7 g Sat); 38 mg Cholesterol; 34 g Carbohydrate; 3 g Fibre; 17 g Protein; 813 mg Sodium

Pictured on page 17.

Lazy Cabbage Roll Casserole

Bacon slices, diced	4	4
Lean ground beef	1 1/2 lbs.	680 g
Chopped onion	1 cup	250 mL
Tomato juice	1 1/4 cups	300 mL
Can of condensed tomato soup	10 oz.	284 mL
Salt	1/2 tsp.	2 mL
Pepper	1/4 tsp.	1 mL
Coarsely shredded cabbage, lightly packed	8 cups	2 L
Long grain white rice	1/3 cup	75 mL

Cook bacon in large frying pan on medium until crisp. Transfer with slotted spoon to paper towels to drain. Set aside.

Heat 2 tsp. (10 mL) drippings in same pan. Add beef and onion. Scramble-fry for about 10 minutes until beef is no longer pink. Drain.

Add next 4 ingredients. Stir. Remove from heat.

Spread cabbage in ungreased 9 x 13 inch (22 x 33 cm) pan. Press down lightly.

Sprinkle bacon and rice over cabbage. Spread beef mixture on top. Cover with greased foil. Bake in 350°F (175°C) oven for about 1 1/2 hours until rice is tender and liquid is absorbed. Serves 6.

1 serving: 316 Calories; 13.0 g Total Fat (5.5 g Mono, 1.2 g Poly, 4.8 g Sat); 60 mg Cholesterol; 25 g Carbohydrate; 3 g Fibre; 25 g Protein; 885 mg Sodium

The perfect answer for busy cooks who want a taste of tradition—without having to spend all day in the kitchen.

about cabbage

When buying cabbage always choose a firm head with tightly wrapped leaves. If a cabbage feels particularly light for its size, it's lost too much of its moisture. Cabbages with loose, withered or discoloured leaves may have been stored too long. Also avoid buying cabbages that have been cut into portions. Once a cabbage has been cut it loses its vitamins and nutrients quickly.

This favourite recipe, with a very cute name, always delivers—and no actual porcupine is required! Be sure to use extra-lean ground beef to avoid excess fat because the meatballs cook right in the stew.

Porcupine Meatball Stew

Large egg	1	1
Fine dry bread crumbs	1/3 cup	75 mL
Finely chopped onion	1/4 cup	60 mL
Garlic clove, minced (or 1/4 tsp., 1 mL, powder)	1	1
Seasoned salt	1 tsp.	5 mL
Pepper	1/8 tsp.	0.5 mL
Extra-lean ground beef	1 lb.	454 g
Long grain white rice	1/4 cup	60 mL
Small onion, cut into 6 wedges	1	1
Medium potatoes, peeled and cubed	2	2
Sliced carrot	2 1/4 cups	550 mL
Diced green pepper	1/2 cup	125 mL
Can of stewed tomatoes (with juice)	14 oz.	398 mL
Water	1/2 cup	125 mL
Beef bouillon powder	1 tsp.	5 mL

Combine first 6 ingredients in medium bowl.

Add beef and rice. Mix well. Roll into 12 balls. Arrange in ungreased 3 quart (3 L) casserole.

Layer next 4 ingredients, in order given, over meatballs.

Combine remaining 3 ingredients in small saucepan. Bring to a boil. Pour over vegetables. Bake, covered, in 325°F (160°C) oven for about 2 hours until meatballs are fully cooked, and internal temperature of beef reaches 160°F (71°C). Serves 4.

1 serving: 558 Calories; 18.3 g Total Fat (7.7 g Mono, 1.2 g Poly, 6.9 g Sat); 146 mg Cholesterol; 57 g Carbohydrate; 7 g Fibre; 41 g Protein; 1331 mg Sodium

Pictured at right.

A rich, creamy casserole topped with fluffy, golden biscuits. Irresistible!

Biscuit-Topped Casserole

Cooking oil	1 tsp.	5 mL
Lean ground beef	1 lb.	454 g
Thinly sliced carrot	1 1/4 cups	300 mL
Chopped onion	3/4 cup	175 mL
Block of cream cheese, softened	4 oz.	125 g
Can of condensed cream of mushroom soup	10 oz.	284 mL
Milk	1/3 cup	75 mL
Salsa (or chili sauce)	1/4 cup	60 mL
Salt	1/2 tsp.	2 mL
Pepper	1/4 tsp.	1 mL
Tube of refrigerator country-style biscuits (10 biscuits per tube)	12 oz.	340 g

Heat cooking oil in large frying pan on medium. Add next 3 ingredients. Scramble-fry for about 10 minutes until beef is no longer pink. Remove from heat. Drain.

Beat cream cheese in large bowl until smooth. Add soup. Stir.

Add beef mixture and next 4 ingredients. Stir. Transfer to ungreased 3 quart (3 L) casserole. Bake, uncovered, in 375°F (190°C) oven for 15 minutes.

Arrange biscuits on beef mixture. Bake, uncovered, for another 20 to 25 minutes until biscuits are golden. Serves 4.

1 serving: 689 Calories; 39.4 g Total Fat (15.6 g Mono, 5.4 g Poly, 15.4 g Sat); 93 mg Cholesterol; 54 g Carbohydrate; 3 g Fibre; 31 g Protein; 2088 mg Sodium

Pictured at right.

Call the tots for taters! Even the youngest members of the family will love this one.

serving suggestion

Balance out your Tater-Topped Beef Bake with a colourful medley of steamed veggies on the side.

Tater-Topped Beef Bake

Cooking oil	1 tsp.	5 mL
Lean ground beef	2 lbs.	900 g
Chopped onion	1 cup	250 mL
Can of condensed cream of mushroom soup	10 oz.	284 mL
Can of condensed cream of chicken soup	10 oz.	284 mL
Milk	1 cup	250 mL
Salt	1 tsp.	5 mL
Pepper	1/4 tsp.	1 mL
Package of frozen potato tots (gems or puffs)	2 1/4 lbs.	1 kg
Grated light sharp Cheddar cheese	1 cup	250 mL

Heat cooking oil in large frying pan on medium. Add beef and onion. Scramble-fry for about 10 minutes until beef is no longer pink. Drain.

Add next 5 ingredients. Stir. Spread in greased 9 x 13 inch (22 x 33 cm) pan.

Arrange potato tots on beef mixture. Bake, uncovered, in 350°F (175°C) oven for 1 hour.

Sprinkle with cheese. Bake for another 10 to 15 minutes until cheese is melted. Serves 8.

1 serving: 526 Calories; 28.5 g Total Fat (11.2 g Mono, 3.2 g Poly, 11.8 g Sat); 67 mg Cholesterol; 40 g Carbohydrate; 4 g Fibre; 29 g Protein; 1784 mg Sodium

Easy Shepherd's Pie

Medium potatoes, peeled and cut up	4	4
Milk	3 – 4 tbsp.	50 – 60 mL
Butter (or hard margarine)	1 tbsp.	15 mL
Seasoned salt	1/2 tsp.	2 mL
Cooking oil	2 tsp.	10 mL
Lean ground beef	1 1/2 lbs.	680 g
Chopped onion	1 cup	250 mL
All-purpose flour	1 tbsp.	15 mL
Salt	1 1/2 tsp.	7 mL
Pepper	1/4 tsp.	1 mL
Milk	1/3 cup	75 mL
Cooked peas	1 cup	250 mL
Cooked sliced carrot	1 cup	250 mL
Ketchup	1 tbsp.	15 mL
Worcestershire sauce	1 tsp.	5 mL
Prepared horseradish	1 tsp.	5 mL
Butter (or hard margarine), melted	2 tbsp.	30 mL
Paprika, sprinkle		

Cook potato in boiling salted water in large saucepan until tender. Drain.

Add next 3 ingredients. Mash. Cover. Set aside.

Heat cooking oil in large frying pan on medium. Add beef and onion. Scramble-fry for about 10 minutes until beef is no longer pink. Drain.

Add next 3 ingredients. Stir.

Slowly add second amount of milk, stirring constantly. Heat and stir for about 2 minutes until boiling and thickened.

Add next 5 ingredients. Stir. Spread in greased 2 quart (2 L) shallow baking dish. Spread mashed potatoes on beef mixture.

Brush with second amount of butter. Sprinkle with paprika. Bake, uncovered, in 350°F (175°C) oven for about 30 minutes until heated through and potatoes are golden. Serves 6.

1 serving: 379 Calories; 17.6 g Total Fat (6.9 g Mono, 1.2 g Poly, 7.8 g Sat); 73 mg Cholesterol; 30 g Carbohydrate; 3.9 g Fibre; 25 g Protein; 915 mg Sodium

Pictured on front cover.

No need for leftover roast beef—you can make this tasty shepherd's pie any day of the week with ground beef.

food fun

Shepherd's pie was originally a British dish made with lamb—hence the name "shepherd!" Although shepherd's pie is still traditionally made with lamb in the United Kingdom, some North Americans may be more familiar with the roast beef version. The leftover roast beef, mashed potatoes, gravy and vegetables from Sunday's dinner were often used to make Monday's shepherd's pie. Nowadays, modern families don't have to wait for leftover roast beef to enjoy this popular dish because ground beef is a tasty and easy substitute.

Apricots, olives and raisins give this meaty casserole an undeniably unique and delicious flavour.

about pimientos

Pimientos are sweet red peppers most commonly seen stuffed inside olives. They are also sold separately in small jars and can be used to add a little extra zip to almost anything, from tuna salad sandwiches to your favourite casserole. Some forms of paprika are made from dried and ground pimientos.

Picadillo Pie

Cooking oil	2 tsp.	10 mL
Lean ground beef	1 1/2 lbs.	680 g
Chopped fresh white mushrooms	1 cup	250 mL
Chopped onion	1 cup	250 mL
Garlic cloves, minced (or 1/2 tsp., 2 mL, powder)	2	2
Chili powder	2 tsp.	10 mL
Ground cumin	1 tsp.	5 mL
Dried oregano	1 tsp.	5 mL
Can of diced tomatoes (with juice)	28 oz.	796 mL
Sliced pimiento-stuffed olives	3/4 cup	175 mL
Chopped dried apricot	1/2 cup	125 mL
Dark raisins	1/2 cup	125 mL
Sweet potatoes (or yams), peeled and cut up	2 lbs.	900 g
Potatoes, peeled and cut up	1 lb.	454 g
Butter (or hard margarine)	3 tbsp.	50 mL
Yellow cornmeal	3 tbsp.	50 mL
Large egg, fork-beaten	1	1
Dried oregano	1/2 tsp.	2 mL
Salt	1/4 tsp.	1 mL
Pepper	1/4 tsp.	1 mL

Heat cooking oil in large frying pan on medium. Add beef. Scramble-fry for about 10 minutes until no longer pink. Drain.

Add next 6 ingredients. Cook for 5 to 10 minutes, stirring occasionally, until onion is softened and liquid is evaporated.

Add next 4 ingredients. Stir. Bring to a boil. Spread in greased 3 quart (3 L) shallow baking dish. Set aside.

Cook sweet potato and potato in boiling salted water in large saucepan until tender. Drain.

(continued on next page)

Add remaining 6 ingredients. Mash. Spread on top of beef mixture. Score decorative pattern on top with a fork. Bake, uncovered, in 375°F (190°C) oven for about 40 minutes until potato mixture is firm. Serves 8.

1 serving: 440 Calories; 15.3 g Total Fat (6.1 g Mono, 1.3 g Poly, 6.1 g Sat); 81 mg Cholesterol; 57 g Carbohydrate; 7 g Fibre; 21 g Protein; 433 mg Sodium

Pictured below.

Top: Hot Tamale Two-Step, page 28
Bottom: Picadillo Pie, page 26

Warm things up with our spicy twist on the tamale pie. Don't let the jalapeño peppers scare you away—their heat is nicely tempered by the cornmeal.

make it a fiesta

Start your meal with some Mexican-style appetizers like nachos or stuffed jalapeños (easily found in your grocer's freezer section). For the main course, serve the Hot Tamale Two-Step casserole and complement it with a fresh salad of crisp greens, bell peppers and crushed taco chips topped with ranch dressing. For added flair, pull out the blender and whip up some frozen margaritas. Olé!

Hot Tamale Two-Step

Cooking oil	2 tsp.	10 mL
Lean ground beef	1 lb.	454 g
Chili powder	1 tbsp.	15 mL
Seasoned salt	2 tsp.	10 mL
Garlic powder	1/2 tsp.	2 mL
Onion powder	1/2 tsp.	2 mL
Large eggs, fork beaten	2	2
Milk	2 cups	500 mL
Frozen kernel corn	2 cups	500 mL
Can of diced tomatoes (with juice)	14 oz.	398 mL
Yellow cornmeal	1 cup	250 mL
Can of sliced jalapeño peppers, drained	4 oz.	114 mL
Grated sharp Cheddar cheese	1 cup	250 mL
Can of sliced black olives, drained	4 1/2 oz.	125 mL

Heat cooking oil in large frying pan on medium. Add beef. Scramble-fry for about 10 minutes until no longer pink. Drain.

Add next 4 ingredients. Heat and stir for about 1 minute until fragrant. Remove from heat.

Combine next 6 ingredients in large bowl. Add beef mixture. Stir. Transfer to greased 2 quart (2 L) casserole. Bake, uncovered, in 375°F (190°C) oven for about 1 hour until firm.

Sprinkle with cheese and olives. Bake for another 5 to 10 minutes until cheese is melted. Serves 6.

1 serving: 441 Calories; 19.2 g Total Fat (7.4 g Mono, 1.7 g Poly, 8.2 g Sat); 134 mg Cholesterol; 41 g Carbohydrate; 4 g Fibre; 28 g Protein; 923 mg Sodium

Pictured on page 27.

Shipwreck

Medium onions, thinly sliced	2	2
Salt (or seasoned salt), sprinkle		
Pepper, sprinkle		
Medium potatoes, peeled and thinly sliced	2	2
Lean ground beef	1 lb.	454 g
Long grain white rice	1/2 cup	125 mL
Chopped celery	1 cup	250 mL
Boiling water	1 1/4 cups	300 mL
Can of condensed tomato soup	10 oz.	284 mL

Put onion into greased 2 1/2 quart (2.5 L) casserole. Sprinkle with salt and pepper.

Layer next 4 ingredients on onion, in order given, sprinkling each layer with salt and pepper.

Combine boiling water and soup in small heatproof bowl. Pour over celery, poking with knife in several places to bottom of casserole to allow soup mixture to flow through. Bake, covered, in 350°F (175°C) oven for 1 1/2 to 2 hours until beef is fully cooked, and internal temperature of beef reaches 160°F (71°C). Serves 4.

1 serving: 509 Calories; 18.7 g Total Fat (7.8 g Mono, 1.5 g Poly, 7.2 g Sat); 64 mg Cholesterol; 58 g Carbohydrate; 4.6 g Fibre; 28 g Protein; 1230 mg Sodium

Pictured on page 31.

The ship may be wrecked but this easy dish will have you sailing on the clear seas! This time-honoured recipe is a favourite with sailors and landlubbers alike.

variations

Casseroles are excellent for experimenting and Shipwreck is no exception. Change the taste by substituting thinly sliced or grated carrot for some of the onion or celery. Add some of your favourite herbs for extra flavour. Also consider designing your own topping. Do you want a little more colour? Or perhaps you desire a satisfying crunch? Personalize your casserole by trying out any of these terrific toppers:

- fresh parsley
- green onions
- sliced or diced tomato
- crumbled potato or nacho chips
- crumbled, cooked bacon
- French-fried onions
- dry chow mein noodles

Baby carrots, potatoes and tender steak make this a most appealing meal!

tip

Consider using less-expensive cuts of beef in dishes that use a tomato-based sauce and require a longer cooking time. The long, slow cooking and the acid in the tomato sauce will tenderize ordinarily tough cuts.

Swiss Steak Casserole

All-purpose flour	1/4 cup	60 mL
Salt	1 tsp.	5 mL
Pepper	1/4 tsp.	1 mL
Beef sirloin tip (or boneless round) steak, cut into 8 equal pieces	2 lbs.	900 g
Cooking oil	1 tbsp.	15 mL
Water	1 cup	250 mL
Can of tomato sauce	7 1/2 oz.	213 mL
Chili sauce	1/2 cup	125 mL
Beef bouillon powder	1 tbsp.	15 mL
Garlic powder	1/4 tsp.	1 mL
Red baby potatoes, larger ones cut in half	2 lbs.	900 g
Bag of baby carrots	1 lb.	454 g
Medium onions, each cut into 8 wedges	2	2

Combine first 3 ingredients in large resealable freezer bag.

Add steak. Seal bag. Toss until coated.

Heat 1 1/2 tsp. (7 mL) of cooking oil in large frying pan on medium-high. Add 4 steak pieces. Cook for 1 to 2 minutes per side until browned. Transfer to medium roasting pan. Repeat with remaining cooking oil and steak.

Combine next 5 ingredients in medium bowl. Pour over steak. Bake, covered, in 300°F (150°C) oven for 1 1/2 hours.

Add remaining 3 ingredients. Stir. Bake, covered, for another 1 1/2 hours until steak and vegetables are tender. Serves 8.

1 serving: 330 Calories; 6.6 g Total Fat (2.8 g Mono, 0.9 g Poly, 1.8 g Sat); 54 mg Cholesterol; 39 g Carbohydrate; 6 g Fibre; 29 g Protein; 1027 mg Sodium

Pictured at right.

Top right: Shipwreck, page 29
Bottom: Swiss Steak Casserole, above

Serve this delicious stew with biscuits to soak up the sauce. Simple to double, or triple, for a crowd—just use a bigger roasting pan.

storing stews

Stew tastes even better on the second day because the flavour develops over time. Cooked stews can be stored, covered, in the refrigerator for up to three days. But don't store your stew for more than a day if it contains fish or shellfish.

Tender beef and veggies are sure to satisfy. A hint of sweetness makes this stew especially appealing.

Oven Stew

Stewing beef, trimmed of fat and cubed	1 lb.	454 g
Medium carrots, cut into 1 inch (2.5 cm) pieces	4	4
Large potatoes, peeled and cubed	2	2
Large onion, chopped	1	1
Can of tomato sauce	7 1/2 oz.	213 mL
Prepared beef broth	1/2 cup	125 mL
Salt	3/4 tsp.	4 mL
Pepper	1/8 tsp.	0.5 mL

Combine all 8 ingredients in ungreased 3 quart (3 L) casserole or small roasting pan. Bake, covered, in 300°F (150°C) oven for 3 1/2 to 4 hours, stirring occasionally, until beef is tender. Serves 4.

1 serving: 320 Calories; 9.4 g Total Fat (3.4 g Mono, 0.6 g Poly, 3.3 g Sat); 61 mg Cholesterol; 27.6 g Carbohydrate; 5 g Fibre; 32 g Protein; 991 mg Sodium

Squash Stew

Butternut squash, peeled and cubed	2 lbs.	900 g
Diced peeled potato	3 cups	750 mL
Sliced carrot	3 cups	750 mL
Stewing beef, trimmed of fat and cubed	1 lb.	454 g
Coarsely chopped onion	1 cup	250 mL
Boiling water	1/2 cup	125 mL
Beef bouillon powder	2 tsp.	10 mL
Can of tomato sauce	7 1/2 oz.	213 mL
Granulated sugar	1/2 tsp.	2 mL
Salt	1/2 tsp.	2 mL
Pepper	1/8 tsp.	0.5 mL

Layer first 5 ingredients, in order given, in ungreased 4 quart (4 L) casserole or medium roasting pan. Set aside.

Measure boiling water into medium heatproof bowl. Add bouillon powder. Stir until dissolved.

(continued on next page)

Add remaining 4 ingredients. Stir. Pour over onion in casserole. Bake, covered, in 300°F (150°C) oven for 3 1/2 to 4 hours until beef and vegetables are tender. Serves 4.

1 serving: 454 Calories; 8.9 g Total Fat (3.2 g Mono, 0.7 g Poly, 3.1 g Sat); 56 mg Cholesterol; 65 g Carbohydrate; 9 g Fibre; 32 g Protein; 1094 mg Sodium

Pictured below.

An attractive and appetizing casserole. Perfect for an autumn day—or any other day for that matter!

Autumn Bake

Medium potatoes, peeled and quartered lengthwise	4	4
All-purpose flour	1/4 cup	60 mL
Salt	3/4 tsp.	4 mL
Pepper	1/4 tsp.	1 mL
Cooking oil	2 tsp.	10 mL
Beef top sirloin steak, cut into thin strips	1 1/4 lbs.	560 g
Salt, sprinkle		
Pepper, sprinkle		
Medium zucchini (with peel), cut into 1/2 inch (12 mm) slices	1	1
Large tomatoes, cut into 1/2 inch (12 mm) slices	2	2
Dried oregano	1/2 tsp.	2 mL
Dried basil	1/2 tsp.	2 mL
Onion powder	1/2 tsp.	2 mL
Butter (or hard margarine)	4 tsp.	20 mL
Grated part-skim mozzarella cheese	1 cup	250 mL
Fine dry bread crumbs	1/2 cup	125 mL

Cook potato in boiling salted water in medium saucepan for about 5 minutes until starting to soften. Drain. Let stand until cool enough to handle. Cut into 1/2 inch (12 mm) slices.

Combine next 3 ingredients in medium bowl. Add potato slices. Toss until coated. Put potato into greased 3 quart (3 L) casserole.

Heat cooking oil in medium frying pan on medium-high. Add beef. Sprinkle with salt and pepper. Heat and stir for about 3 minutes until browned. Scatter over potato.

Layer zucchini and tomato slices on beef.

Combine next 3 ingredients in small cup. Sprinkle over tomato slices.

(continued on next page)

Melt butter in small saucepan. Remove from heat. Add cheese and bread crumbs. Stir until well mixed. Sprinkle over top. Bake, uncovered, in 350°F (175°C) oven for about 1 hour until golden and heated through. Serves 4.

1 serving: 627 Calories; 25.0 g Total Fat (9.6 g Mono, 1.9 g Poly, 11.0 g Sat); 99 mg Cholesterol; 58 g Carbohydrate; 5 g Fibre; 42 g Protein; 847 mg Sodium

Pictured below.

When you're in the mood for something spicy, this one-dish meal is just the ticket!

West Indies Beef

All-purpose flour	1/3 cup	75 mL
Seasoned salt	1 tsp.	5 mL
Paprika	1 tsp.	5 mL
Pepper	1/2 tsp.	2 mL
Beef inside round (or boneless beef blade) steak, trimmed of fat and cut into 3/4 inch (2 cm) cubes	2 lbs.	900 g
Cooking oil	2 tbsp.	30 mL
Chopped onion	1 1/2 cups	375 mL
Water	2 tbsp.	30 mL
Garlic cloves, minced (or 1/2 tsp., 2 mL, powder)	2	2
Chopped tomato	2 cups	500 mL
Chopped green pepper	1 cup	250 mL
Finely grated gingerroot (or 1 tsp., 5 mL, ground ginger)	1 tbsp.	15 mL
Ground cumin	1/2 tsp.	2 mL
Cayenne pepper	1/4 tsp.	1 mL
Water	2 1/2 cups	625 mL
Long grain white rice	1 cup	250 mL
Salt	1 tsp.	5 mL

Combine first 4 ingredients in large resealable freezer bag.

Add beef. Seal bag. Toss until coated.

Heat cooking oil in large frying pan on medium-high. Add beef in 3 batches. Cook for about 5 minutes per batch until beef is browned on all sides. Transfer with slotted spoon to ungreased 3 quart (3 L) casserole.

Heat and stir next 3 ingredients in same pan for about 5 minutes, scraping any brown bits from bottom of pan, until onion starts to soften. Add to beef.

Add next 5 ingredients. Stir. Bake, covered, in 325°F (160°C) oven for about 1 1/2 hours until beef is tender.

(continued on next page)

Combine remaining 3 ingredients in medium saucepan. Bring to a boil. Reduce heat to medium-low. Simmer, uncovered, for about 10 minutes, without stirring, until rice is partially cooked. Do not drain. Add to beef mixture. Stir. Bake, covered, for another 30 to 40 minutes until rice is tender and liquid is absorbed. Serves 6.

1 serving: 399 Calories; 8.4 g Total Fat (4.1 g Mono, 1.7 g Poly, 1.5 g Sat); 65 mg Cholesterol; 40 g Carbohydrate; 2.2 g Fibre; 39 g Protein; 685 mg Sodium

Pictured below.

Prepare today to bake tomorrow. If you enjoy the taste of Reuben sandwiches, you'll love this casserole combination of corned beef, sauerkraut and Swiss cheese.

food fun

Two competing stories claim to tell the true origin of the Reuben sandwich. The first asserts that the Reuben was first served in a Manhattan deli named Reuben's. Allegedly, the sandwich was designed in 1918 for one of Charlie Chaplin's leading ladies. The second story claims that grocer Reuben Kulakofsky whipped up the sandwich to feed hungry poker-playing patrons at the Blackstone Hotel in Omaha.

Reuben Bake

Dijon mustard	2 tbsp.	30 mL
Rye bread slices (about 1/4 inch, 6 mm, thick)	10	10
Deli corned beef, cut into thin strips	12 1/2 oz.	350 g
Jar of sauerkraut, rinsed and drained well	17 1/2 oz.	500 mL
Grated Swiss (or medium Cheddar) cheese	2 cups	500 mL
Large eggs	6	6
Milk	2 1/2 cups	625 mL
Green onion, sliced	1	1
Pepper	1/4 tsp.	1 mL

Spread mustard on 1 side of bread slices. Cut into cubes. Spread in greased 9 x 13 inch (22 x 33 cm) pan.

Layer corned beef and sauerkraut on bread. Sprinkle with cheese.

Beat remaining 4 ingredients in medium bowl until combined. Pour over cheese. Cover with greased foil. Chill for at least 6 hours or overnight. Bake, covered, in 350°F (175°C) oven for 40 minutes. Bake, uncovered, for another 35 to 40 minutes until bubbling and cheese is golden. Serves 8.

1 serving: 395 Calories;18.7 g Total Fat (6.6 g Mono, 1.5 g Poly, 8.6 g Sat); 234 mg Cholesterol; 28 g Carbohydrate; 4 g Fibre; 28 g Protein; 1277 mg Sodium

Chicken Divan

Water	2 cups	500 mL
Vegetable bouillon powder	2 tsp.	10 mL
Boneless, skinless chicken breast halves	1 1/2 lbs.	680 g
Water	2 1/2 cups	625 mL
Long grain white rice	1 1/4 cups	300 mL
Frozen chopped broccoli, chopped smaller	1 lb.	454 g
Can of condensed cream of chicken soup	10 oz.	284 mL
Light sour cream	1/2 cup	125 mL
Grated medium Cheddar cheese	1/2 cup	125 mL
Water	1/2 cup	125 mL
Light salad dressing (or mayonnaise)	1/3 cup	75 mL
Curry powder	1 tsp.	5 mL

Combine first amount of water and bouillon powder in medium saucepan. Bring to a boil. Add chicken. Reduce heat to medium-low. Simmer, partially covered, for about 35 minutes until no longer pink inside. Drain. Let chicken stand until cool enough to handle. Cut into cubes. Set aside.

Combine second amount of water and rice in same saucepan. Bring to a boil. Reduce heat to medium-low. Simmer, covered, for about 20 minutes until rice is tender and water is absorbed. Transfer to ungreased 3 quart (3 L) casserole.

Layer broccoli and chicken on rice.

Combine remaining 6 ingredients in medium bowl. Pour over chicken. Bake, uncovered, in 350°F (175°C) oven for about 1 hour until heated through. Serves 6.

1 serving: 470 Calories; 14.1 g Total Fat (5.8 g Mono, 2.5 g Poly, 5.6 g Sat); 100 mg Cholesterol; 43 g Carbohydrate; 2 g Fibre; 41 g Protein; 598 mg Sodium

Pictured on page 41.

This Divan is simply divine! You'll love the delicate curry flavour.

tip

Never substitute non-fat sour cream in a cooked recipe that calls for light or regular sour cream—it can negatively effect taste and texture.

Literally "rice with chicken," Arroz Con Pollo (ah-ROHS con POH-yoh) is a Latin American dish your family will ask for often. Saffron may be a bit more expensive than other spices but it adds a special touch.

about saffron

Generally produced in the Mediterranean and India, over 5200 saffron crocus flowers must be hand-picked, dried and processed to make only one ounce of saffron! This labour-intensive process is the reason why saffron is the most expensive spice in the world. But lucky for us, only a little is needed to impart a vibrant golden colour and add a distinct flavour to dishes. To ensure you're spending your money wisely and getting the genuine article, buy whole stigmas (threadlike filaments) rather than ground saffron. Turmeric may be used as a substitute—it will give a dish the same vibrant yellow colour but will impart a different flavour.

Arroz Con Pollo

Ingredient	Imperial	Metric
Bone-in chicken parts, skin removed (see Note)	3 1/2 lbs.	1.6 kg
Boiling water	3 cups	750 mL
Frozen peas	2 cups	500 mL
Can of diced tomatoes (with juice)	14 oz.	398 mL
Long grain white rice	1 1/2 cups	375 mL
Finely chopped onion	1/2 cup	125 mL
Jar of pimiento, well drained and chopped	2 oz.	57 mL
Chicken bouillon powder	1 tbsp.	15 mL
Dried basil	1/2 tsp.	2 mL
Salt	1 tsp.	5 mL
Pepper	1/4 tsp.	1 mL
Saffron threads (or turmeric)	1/4 tsp.	1 mL
Garlic powder	1/4 tsp.	1 mL

Arrange chicken in greased 9 x 13 inch (22 x 33 cm) pan. Bake, uncovered, in 350°F (175°C) oven for 30 minutes. Transfer to large plate.

Combine remaining 12 ingredients in same pan. Arrange chicken on rice mixture. Cover with greased foil. Bake for another 35 to 45 minutes until chicken is no longer pink inside, rice is tender and liquid is absorbed. Serves 6.

1 serving: 396 Calories; 4.9 g Total Fat (1.4 g Mono, 1.3 g Poly, 1.2 g Sat); 90 mg Cholesterol; 51 g Carbohydrate; 4 g Fibre; 35 g Protein; 990 mg Sodium

Pictured at right.

Note: Use whichever cut of chicken you prefer as long as the weight used is equal to that listed.

Top: Chicken Divan, page 39
Bottom: Arroz Con Pollo, above

A time-honoured casserole sure to win compliments for the cook! Put this together in only ten minutes, and toss a salad or steam some vegetables while it bakes.

about brown and white rice

So what is the difference between brown and white rice? Brown rice is considered whole grain rice because only the outer husk is removed, leaving a brown bran layer. White rice has the bran layer removed during the milling process. Brown rice is more nutritious because it contains extra nutrients and fibre in the bran layer. Remember: white and brown rice cannot always be easily interchanged in dishes—their tastes and cooking times are different!

If you're having a busy day, give yourself a break with this easy-to-prepare casserole. Add a bit of cucumber or tomato to a packaged salad for a quick side dish.

Chicken 'N' Rice

Boiling water	3 cups	750 mL
Long grain brown rice	1 1/2 cups	375 mL
Dehydrated mixed vegetables	2/3 cup	150 mL
Chicken bouillon powder	1 tbsp.	15 mL
Poultry seasoning	1/2 tsp.	2 mL
Celery salt	1/2 tsp.	2 mL
Dried rosemary, crushed	1/4 tsp.	1 mL
Garlic clove, minced (or 1/4 tsp., 1 mL, powder), optional	1	1
Bone-in chicken parts, skin removed (see Note)	3 1/2 lbs.	1.6 kg
Paprika	1/2 tsp.	2 mL
Pepper	1/4 tsp.	1 mL

Combine first 8 ingredients in greased 9 x 13 inch (22 x 33 cm) baking dish.

Arrange chicken on rice mixture. Do not stir. Sprinkle with paprika and pepper. Cover with greased foil. Bake in 350°F (175°C) oven for about 1 1/2 hours until chicken is no longer pink inside, rice is tender and liquid is absorbed. Serves 6.

1 serving: 371 Calories; 5.8 g Total Fat (1.8 g Mono, 1.7 g Poly, 1.4 g Sat); 90 mg Cholesterol; 45 g Carbohydrate; 2 g Fibre; 33 g Protein; 626 mg Sodium

Note: Use whichever cut of chicken you prefer as long as the weight used is equal to that listed.

Handy Dandy Chicken

Instant white rice	2 cups	500 mL
Can of mushroom stems and pieces, drained	10 oz.	284 mL
Can of condensed cream of mushroom soup	10 oz.	284 mL
Can of condensed cream of chicken soup	10 oz.	284 mL
Apple juice	3/4 cup	175 mL
Envelope of vegetable soup mix	1 1/4 oz.	40 g
Bone-in chicken parts, skin removed (see Note)	3 lbs.	1.4 kg

(continued on next page)

Combine first 6 ingredients in large bowl. Spread in ungreased 9 x 13 inch (22 x 33 cm) pan.

Arrange chicken, meaty-side up, on rice mixture. Cover with greased foil. Bake in 350°F (175°C) oven for 1 1/2 to 2 hours until chicken is no longer pink inside. Serves 6.

1 serving: 401 Calories; 10.7 g Total Fat (3.2 g Mono, 3.3 g Poly, 2.9 g Sat); 83 mg Cholesterol; 44 g Carbohydrate; 2 g Fibre; 30 g Protein; 1439 mg Sodium

Pictured below.

Note: Use whichever cut of chicken you prefer as long as the weight used is equal to that listed.

Chicken and beans are slowly baked to tender perfection in a fragrant tomato broth. Lemon and parsley add a fresh touch. Ideal for a relaxed dinner with friends.

Mediterranean Chicken And Bean Casserole

Dried navy beans	2 1/3 cups	575 mL
Olive (or cooking) oil	1 tbsp.	15 mL
Bone-in chicken thighs (5 – 6 oz., 140 – 170 g, each), skin removed	8	8
Chopped onion	2 cups	500 mL
Chopped fennel bulb (white part only), or chopped celery	1 cup	250 mL
Low-sodium prepared chicken broth	3 cups	750 mL
Can of diced tomatoes (with juice)	14 oz.	398 mL
Garlic cloves, minced	6	6
Bay leaves	2	2
Pepper	1 tsp.	5 mL
Medium lemon, cut into 8 slices	1	1
Chopped fresh parsley	1/2 cup	125 mL
Salt	1 tsp.	5 mL

Measure beans into large bowl. Cover with water. Soak for at least 8 hours or overnight. Drain. Transfer to greased 4 quart (4 L) casserole or medium roasting pan.

Heat olive oil in large frying pan on medium-high. Add chicken. Cook for about 5 minutes per side until browned. Transfer to large plate. Set aside.

Cook onion and fennel in same pan for 5 to 10 minutes, stirring often, until onion is softened. Add to beans in casserole. Stir.

Add next 5 ingredients. Stir. Press chicken into bean mixture.

Top with lemon slices. Bake, covered, in 350°F (175°C) oven for about 3 1/2 hours until beans are softened. Discard lemon slices and bay leaves. Remove chicken to large serving platter.

Add parsley and salt to bean mixture. Stir. Serve with chicken. Serves 8.

1 serving: 329 Calories; 6.1 g Total Fat (2.4 g Mono, 1.4 g Poly, 1.3 g Sat); 52 mg Cholesterol; 43 g Carbohydrate; 11 g Fibre; 27 g Protein; 636 mg Sodium

Pictured at right and on back cover.

Make your chicken pie and eat it too! Similar to a chicken pot pie, but lower in sodium—and there's no hassle of having to make a crust!

food fun

Did you know that garlic is considered nature's antibiotic? From the elegant ancient Egyptians to the godly Ancient Greeks, people throughout the ages have used garlic to treat many ailments. Even the father of antibiotic medicine, Louis Pasteur, studied the pungent plant. Pasteur noticed that some bacteria were killed when they came in contact with the "stinking rose." Although nowhere near as potent as medical antibiotics (and not to be substituted for them!), garlic supplements are taken by many people for their purported health benefits.

Crustless Chicken Pie

Cooking oil	3 tbsp.	50 mL
Boneless, skinless chicken breast halves, cut into 1 inch (2.5 cm) pieces	1 lb.	454 g
Original no-salt seasoning (such as Mrs. Dash)	1 tsp.	5 mL
Chopped celery	1 cup	250 mL
Chopped onion	3/4 cup	175 mL
Garlic cloves, minced (or 1/2 tsp., 2 mL, powder)	2	2
Chopped peeled potato	1 cup	250 mL
Chopped green pepper	2/3 cup	150 mL
Chopped red pepper	2/3 cup	150 mL
Bay leaf	1	1
Dried savory	1/2 tsp.	2 mL
All-purpose flour	3 tbsp.	50 mL
Low-sodium prepared chicken broth	1 cup	250 mL
Light sour cream	1/4 cup	60 mL
Grated light medium Cheddar cheese	1/2 cup	125 mL
Grated Swiss cheese	1/2 cup	125 mL

Chopped fresh parsley, for garnish

Heat cooking oil in large frying pan on medium-high. Add chicken. Sprinkle with seasoning. Cook for about 5 minutes, stirring occasionally, until no longer pink inside. Transfer with slotted spoon to medium bowl. Set aside. Reduce heat to medium.

Cook celery and onion in same pan for 5 to 10 minutes, stirring often, until softened.

Add garlic. Heat and stir for 1 to 2 minutes until fragrant.

Add chicken and next 5 ingredients. Stir.

(continued on next page)

Measure flour into small bowl. Slowly add broth, stirring constantly until smooth. Slowly add to chicken mixture, stirring constantly until boiling and thickened. Reduce heat to medium-low. Simmer, covered, for about 25 minutes, stirring occasionally, until potato is tender. Discard bay leaf.

Add sour cream. Stir. Transfer to greased 2 quart (2 L) casserole.

Sprinkle with both cheeses. Bake, uncovered, in 425°F (220°C) oven for about 20 minutes until cheese is melted.

Garnish with parsley. Serves 4.

1 serving: 423 Calories; 21 g Total Fat (9.2 g Mono, 3.9 g Poly, 7.1 g Sat); 91 mg Cholesterol; 22 g Carbohydrate; 3 g Fibre; 37 g Protein; 331 mg Sodium

Pictured below.

Make it easy on yourself and use ready-made pastry for the quickest preparation of this family favourite.

tip

If a recipe calls for leftover gravy and there isn't a drop in sight, you can use store-bought canned gravy. Or, if the dish uses chicken, you can substitute the gravy with a can of cream of chicken soup or mushroom soup and add 3/4 cup (175 mL) water.

Chicken Pot Pie

Diced cooked chicken	3 cups	750 mL
Can of sliced mushrooms, drained	10 oz.	284 mL
Frozen peas	1 cup	250 mL
Chopped peeled potato	2 cups	500 mL
Sliced carrot	2 cups	500 mL
Chopped onion	1/2 cup	125 mL
Chicken gravy	2 cups	500 mL
Onion powder	1/4 tsp.	1 mL
Celery salt	1/4 tsp.	1 mL

Pastry for 9 inch (22 cm) deep dish pie shell, your own or a mix

Combine first 3 ingredients in ungreased 3 quart (3 L) casserole.

Cook next 3 ingredients in boiling salted water in medium saucepan until vegetables are tender. Drain. Add to chicken mixture. Stir.

Heat next 3 ingredients in same saucepan. Add a little water, if needed, to thin gravy. Pour over chicken mixture, lifting with a fork in several places to allow gravy to flow through.

Roll out pastry about 1/2 inch (12 mm) larger than top of casserole. Place on chicken mixture, pressing edge of pastry up sides of casserole. Cut 2 or 3 small slits in pastry to allow steam to escape. Bake, uncovered, in 400°F (205°C) oven for about 30 minutes until pastry is golden. Serves 6.

1 serving: 441 Calories; 18.9 g Total Fat (8.8 g Mono, 3.7 g Poly, 4.9 g Sat); 69 mg Cholesterol; 39 g Carbohydrate; 5 g Fibre; 29 g Protein; 963 mg Sodium

Pictured at right.

Tender dumplings rest on a creamy base of chicken and ham. A great dish when you're in need of a little comfort.

about mushrooms

There are many types of mushrooms available today with a wide range of tastes, textures and colours. Generally, the most commonly found variety is the white mushroom, also known as a button mushroom when younger and smaller in size. Other types of mushrooms you might find at your local grocer's include the portobello, shiitake, oyster and crimini, among many others. So don't leave all the other mushrooms in the dark! Venture away from white mushrooms, and try something new!

Dumpling Casserole

Cooking oil	1 tbsp.	15 mL
Chopped onion	1 cup	250 mL
Chopped celery	1 cup	250 mL
Sliced fresh white mushrooms	1 cup	250 mL
All-purpose flour	1/4 cup	60 mL
Chicken bouillon powder	2 tsp.	10 mL
Seasoned salt	1/2 tsp.	2 mL
Pepper	1/4 tsp.	1 mL
Milk	1 1/2 cups	375 mL
Water	1 cup	250 mL
Cubed cooked chicken	3 cups	750 mL
Cubed cooked ham	1 cup	250 mL
SWEET POTATO DUMPLINGS		
All-purpose flour	1 1/2 cups	375 mL
Baking powder	1 tbsp.	15 mL
Salt	1/2 tsp.	2 mL
Ground nutmeg	1/4 tsp.	1 mL
Ground cinnamon	1/4 tsp.	1 mL
Large egg	1	1
Mashed sweet potatoes (see Note) (about 1/2 lb., 225 g, uncooked)	2 cups	500 mL
Milk	1/2 cup	125 mL
Cooking oil	1/3 cup	75 mL

Heat cooking oil in large frying pan on medium. Add onion and celery. Cook for 5 minutes, stirring occasionally.

Add mushrooms. Cook for another 4 to 5 minutes, stirring occasionally, until onion and mushrooms are softened.

Combine next 4 ingredients in small bowl. Slowly add milk, stirring constantly until smooth. Add water. Stir. Slowly add to mushroom mixture, stirring constantly until boiling and thickened.

Combine chicken and ham in ungreased 3 quart (3 L) casserole. Add mushroom mixture. Stir. Bake, covered, in 400°F (205°C) oven for 15 minutes.

(continued on next page)

Sweet Potato Dumplings: Measure first 5 ingredients into medium bowl. Stir. Make a well in centre.

Combine remaining 4 ingredients in small bowl. Add to well. Stir until just moistened. Drop by spoonfuls on chicken mixture in casserole to make 8 dumplings. Bake, uncovered, for another 45 to 50 minutes until dumplings are golden and wooden pick inserted in centre of dumpling comes out clean. Serves 8.

1 serving: 490 Calories; 19.3 g Total Fat (9.5 g Mono, 5.0 g Poly, 3.3 g Sat); 91 mg Cholesterol; 50 g Carbohydrate; 4 g Fibre; 29 g Protein; 917 mg Sodium

Pictured below.

Note: Only sweet potatoes with a pale yellow interior will have the drier texture that is required. To ensure you are purchasing the correct product, pierce the skin of the sweet potato with your fingernail so you can see the colour of the inner flesh. Ensure the interior is pale yellow rather than dark orange.

Delightfully different! A delicate mushroom wine sauce coats tender pasta while sun-dried tomatoes and artichokes lend a tangy touch to each bite.

Riviera Chicken Casserole

Rotini (or other spiral) pasta	2 cups	500 mL
Sun-dried tomatoes	4	4
Cooking oil	2 tsp.	10 mL
Sliced fresh white mushrooms	3 cups	750 mL
Thinly sliced leek (white part only)	1 3/4 cups	425 mL
Can of condensed chicken broth	10 oz.	284 mL
Dry (or alcohol-free) white wine	1/2 cup	125 mL
Water	1/2 cup	125 mL
Cornstarch	2 tbsp.	30 mL
Chopped cooked chicken	3 cups	750 mL
Can of artichoke hearts, drained and chopped	14 oz.	398 mL
Grated Swiss cheese	1/2 cup	125 mL
Chopped fresh parsley	1/4 cup	60 mL

Cook pasta in boiling salted water in large uncovered saucepan or Dutch oven for 8 to 10 minutes, stirring occasionally, until tender but firm. Drain. Return to same saucepan. Set aside.

Put sun-dried tomatoes into small saucepan. Cover with water. Bring to a boil. Boil gently on medium for about 10 minutes until softened. Drain. Chop finely. Add to pasta. Stir.

Heat cooking oil in large frying pan on medium. Add mushrooms and leek. Cook for 5 to 10 minutes, stirring occasionally, until softened and liquid is evaporated.

Add broth and wine. Stir.

Combine water and cornstarch in small cup. Slowly add to broth mixture, stirring constantly until smooth. Heat and stir for about 1 minute until boiling and thickened. Add to pasta mixture. Stir.

Add next 3 ingredients. Stir. Transfer to greased 3 quart (3 L) casserole. Bake, covered, in 375°F (190°C) oven for about 30 minutes until heated through.

Sprinkle with parsley. Serves 6.

1 serving: 412 Calories; 10.1 g Total Fat (3.7 g Mono, 2.3 g Poly, 2.9 g Sat); 73 mg Cholesterol; 42 g Carbohydrate; 4 g Fibre; 35 g Protein; 560 mg Sodium

Pictured at right.

Named after opera singer Luisa Tetrazzini, this version of the traditionally rich dish is light enough to have you easily hitting the high notes.

Chicken Tetrazzini

Water	2 cups	500 mL
Bone-in chicken breast halves, skin removed	1 1/2 lbs.	680 g
Spaghetti, broken up	1/2 lb.	225 g
Cooking oil	2 tsp.	10 mL
Sliced fresh white mushrooms	2 cups	500 mL
Sliced red pepper	1/2 cup	125 mL
Sliced green onion	1/3 cup	75 mL
All-purpose flour	2 tbsp.	30 mL
Low-sodium chicken bouillon powder	2 tsp.	10 mL
Water	1/4 cup	60 mL
Skim evaporated milk	1/2 cup	125 mL
Grated Parmesan cheese	1/3 cup	75 mL
Medium sherry	2 tbsp.	30 mL
Salt	1/4 tsp.	1 mL
Pepper	1/8 tsp.	0.5 mL
Grated light sharp Cheddar cheese	1 cup	250 mL

Measure first amount of water into medium saucepan. Bring to a boil. Add chicken. Boil, partially covered, for about 30 minutes until no longer pink inside. Drain and reserve broth. You should have 3/4 to 1 cup (175 to 250 mL). Let chicken stand until cool enough to handle. Discard bones. Cut chicken into cubes. Set aside.

Cook spaghetti in boiling salted water in large uncovered saucepan or Dutch oven for 8 to 10 minutes, stirring occasionally, until tender but firm. Drain. Add chicken. Toss. Set aside.

Heat cooking oil in large frying pan on medium. Add next 3 ingredients. Cook for about 10 minutes, stirring occasionally, until red pepper is softened.

Combine flour and bouillon powder in small bowl. Slowly add second amount of water, stirring constantly until smooth. Add reserved broth. Stir. Slowly add to red pepper mixture, stirring constantly. Heat and stir for about 1 minute until boiling and thickened.

(continued on next page)

Add next 5 ingredients. Stir. Add to spaghetti mixture. Toss. Transfer to greased 3 quart (3 L) casserole. Bake, covered, in 350°F (175°C) oven for about 30 minutes until heated through.

Sprinkle with Cheddar cheese. Bake, uncovered, for another 4 to 5 minutes until cheese is melted. Serves 4.

1 serving: 561 Calories; 14.4 g Total Fat (4.6 g Mono, 1.9 g Poly, 6.4 g Sat); 96 mg Cholesterol; 54 g Carbohydrate; 2 g Fibre; 49 g Protein; 761 mg Sodium

Pictured below.

This rich and cheesy dish is fit for a Tsar—or Tsarina. Pairs excellently with a Caesar salad—a noble meal, indeed!

tip

Don't have any leftover chicken? Start with 2 boneless, skinless chicken breast halves (4 – 6 oz.,113 – 170 g, each). Place in a large frying pan with 1 cup (250 mL) water or chicken broth. Simmer, covered, for 12 to 14 minutes until no longer pink inside. Drain. Chop. Makes about 2 cups (750 mL) of cooked chicken.

Chicken Noodles Romanoff

Medium egg noodles	5 cups	1.25 L
Chopped cooked chicken	2 cups	500 mL
Sour cream	1 cup	250 mL
2% cottage cheese	1 cup	250 mL
Grated sharp Cheddar cheese	1/2 cup	125 mL
Onion flakes	1 tbsp.	15 mL
Worcestershire sauce	1/2 tsp.	2 mL
Salt	1/2 tsp.	2 mL
Hot pepper sauce	1/4 tsp.	1 mL
Garlic powder	1/4 tsp.	1 mL
Grated sharp Cheddar cheese	1/2 cup	125 mL

Cook noodles in boiling salted water in large uncovered saucepan or Dutch oven for 6 to 8 minutes, stirring occasionally, until tender but firm. Drain. Return to same saucepan.

Add next 9 ingredients. Stir. Transfer to greased 3 quart (3 L) casserole.

Sprinkle with second amount of Cheddar cheese. Bake, uncovered, in 350°F (175°C) oven for 30 to 40 minutes until heated through. Serves 6.

1 serving: 418 Calories; 18.3 g Total Fat (5.5 g Mono, 1.7 g Poly, 9.6 g Sat); 120 mg Cholesterol; 31 g Carbohydrate; 1 g Fibre; 32 g Protein; 561 mg Sodium

Pictured at right.

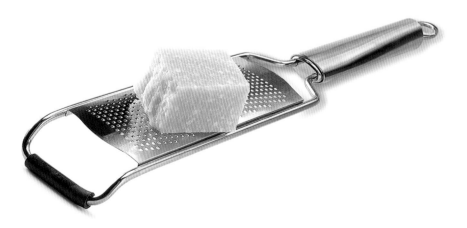

Peppers, mushrooms and tender chicken in a thick tomato sauce flavoured with garlic and wine.

storing dried herbs

Sorry to say, but dried basil that has been sitting, neglected, in your cupboard for 20 years has probably lost its potency. Dried herbs can go stale quickly. Look for dried herbs that are green in colour and give off a strong aroma when crushed between your fingers. Keep your dried herbs fresh longer by storing them in a cool, dark place in airtight containers.

Cacciatore Casserole

Ingredient	Imperial	Metric
Broad egg noodles	5 cups	1.25 L
Olive (or cooking) oil	1 tsp.	5 mL
Sliced fresh white mushrooms	1 cup	250 mL
Diced green pepper	1/2 cup	125 mL
Diced onion	1/2 cup	125 mL
Garlic clove, minced (or 1/4 tsp., 1 mL, powder)	1	1
Olive (or cooking) oil	1 tsp.	5 mL
Boneless, skinless chicken breast halves, thinly sliced	1/2 lb.	225 g
Pepper	1/8 tsp.	0.5 mL
Can of stewed tomatoes (with juice), mashed	14 oz.	398 mL
Prepared chicken broth	1 cup	250 mL
Can of tomato paste	5 1/2 oz.	156 mL
Dry (or alcohol-free) red wine	1/4 cup	60 mL
Granulated sugar	1 tsp.	5 mL
Dried basil	1 tsp.	5 mL
Dried oregano	1 tsp.	5 mL
Bay leaf	1	1
Grated part-skim mozzarella cheese	3/4 cup	175 mL
Grated Parmesan cheese	2 tbsp.	30 mL

Chopped fresh parsley, for garnish

Cook noodles in boiling salted water in large uncovered saucepan or Dutch oven for 6 to 8 minutes, stirring occasionally, until tender but firm. Drain. Return to same saucepan. Set aside.

Heat first amount of olive oil in large frying pan on medium-high. Add next 4 ingredients. Cook for 5 to 10 minutes, stirring often, until onion is softened. Transfer to medium bowl.

Heat second amount of olive oil in same pan. Add chicken. Sprinkle with pepper. Cook for about 5 minutes, stirring occasionally, until no longer pink inside. Add to mushroom mixture. Stir. Set aside.

(continued on next page)

Heat and stir next 4 ingredients in same pan, scraping any brown bits from bottom of pan, until combined.

Add next 4 ingredients. Stir. Bring to a boil. Add chicken mixture. Stir. Reduce heat to medium-low. Simmer, uncovered, for about 15 minutes until sauce is thickened. Discard bay leaf. Add to noodles. Stir. Transfer to greased 2 quart (2 L) casserole.

Sprinkle with both cheeses. Bake, covered, in 350°F (175°C) oven for 25 to 30 minutes until heated through and cheese is bubbling.

Garnish with parsley. Serves 4.

1 serving: 484 Calories; 11.4 g Total Fat (4.2 g Mono, 1.6 g Poly, 4.2 g Sat); 102 mg Cholesterol; 63 g Carbohydrate; 6 g Fibre; 32 g Protein; 688 mg Sodium

Pictured below.

Crunchy noodles top this casserole seasoned with five-spice powder.

Oriental Rice Casserole

Cooking oil	2 tsp.	10 mL
Lean ground chicken (or turkey)	1 lb.	454 g
Chopped onion	1 cup	250 mL
Thinly sliced celery	1 cup	250 mL
Diced red pepper	1 cup	250 mL
Frozen peas	2 cups	500 mL
Fresh bean sprouts	1 1/2 cups	375 mL
Long grain white rice	1 1/2 cups	375 mL
Can of sliced mushrooms (with liquid)	10 oz.	284 mL
Soy sauce	3 tbsp.	50 mL
Can of condensed cream of mushroom soup	10 oz.	284 mL
Hot water	1 cup	250 mL
Oyster sauce	1 tbsp.	15 mL
Chinese five-spice powder	1/2 tsp.	2 mL
Pepper	1/2 tsp.	2 mL
Dry chow mein noodles	1 cup	250 mL

Heat cooking oil in large frying pan on medium-high. Add next 4 ingredients. Scramble-fry for about 10 minutes until chicken is no longer pink. Drain.

Add next 5 ingredients. Stir. Remove from heat.

Combine next 5 ingredients in 4 quart (4 L) casserole or medium roasting pan. Add chicken mixture. Stir. Bake, covered, in 350°F (175°C) oven for about 45 minutes, stirring once at halftime, until rice is tender and liquid is absorbed.

Just before serving, sprinkle with noodles. Serves 6.

1 serving: 517 Calories; 18.8 g Total Fat (2.4 g Mono, 3.9 g Poly, 1.7 g Sat); 1 mg Cholesterol; 64 g Carbohydrate; 5.4 g Fibre; 24 g Protein; 1354 mg Sodium

Pictured at right.

You won't have any difficulties using up your leftover turkey when you've got this recipe! A yummy casserole that's sure to disappear quickly.

Creamed Turkey Noodle

Broad egg noodles	4 cups	1 L
Butter (or hard margarine)	2 tbsp.	30 mL
Chopped celery	2 cups	500 mL
Chopped onion	1 1/2 cups	375 mL
Diced cooked turkey	4 cups	1 L
Can of condensed cream of mushroom soup	10 oz.	284 mL
Can of condensed cream of chicken soup	10 oz.	284 mL
Can of sliced mushrooms, drained	10 oz.	284 mL
Pepper	1/4 tsp.	1 mL

Cook noodles in boiling salted water in large uncovered saucepan or Dutch oven for 6 to 8 minutes, stirring occasionally, until tender but firm. Drain. Return to same saucepan. Set aside.

Melt butter in medium frying pan on medium. Add celery and onion. Cook for 5 to 10 minutes, stirring often, until softened. Add to noodles.

Combine remaining 5 ingredients in ungreased 3 quart (3 L) casserole. Add noodle mixture. Stir. Bake, uncovered, in 350°F (175°C) oven for about 35 minutes until heated through. Serves 6.

1 serving: 402 Calories; 13.1 g Total Fat (3.7 g Mono, 3.2 g Poly, 4.9 g Sat); 123 mg Cholesterol; 34 g Carbohydrate; 3 g Fibre; 36 g Protein; 1038 mg Sodium

Pictured at right.

Top: Bean And Turkey Bake, page 65
Bottom: Creamed Turkey Noodle, above

Reminiscent of lazy cabbage rolls—spiced up southern style! Add extra cayenne pepper for an even spicier flavour.

freezer tomatoes

When you freeze ripe tomatoes they retain their fresh, sweet flavour. If you grow tomatoes in your garden, try freezing some to enjoy during the winter months in soups, stews and casseroles. Follow these simple steps:

1. Peel and quarter tomatoes.
2. Quickly bring to a boil in a saucepan and simmer on medium-low for 5 to 10 minutes.
3. Place the saucepan in a sink of ice water so that the water level sits just below the edge of the pan.
4. Once the tomatoes have cooled completely, transfer them to an airtight container.
5. Label the containers and freeze.

Southern Turkey Casserole

Butter (or hard margarine)	2 tbsp.	30 mL
Chopped onion	3/4 cup	175 mL
Tomato juice	3 cups	750 mL
Chopped green cabbage	3 cups	750 mL
Chopped cooked turkey	2 cups	500 mL
Can of stewed tomatoes (with juice), broken up	14 oz.	398 mL
Long grain white rice	1 cup	250 mL
Parsley flakes	2 tsp.	10 mL
Salt	1 tsp.	5 mL
Pepper	1/4 tsp.	1 mL
Garlic powder	1/2 tsp.	2 mL
Cayenne pepper	1/8 tsp.	0.5 mL

Melt butter in large frying pan on medium. Add onion. Cook for 5 to 10 minutes, stirring often, until softened. Transfer to greased 3 quart (3 L) casserole.

Add remaining 10 ingredients. Stir. Casserole will be full, but turkey mixture will reduce slightly when cooked. Bake, covered, in 350°F (175°C) oven for about 1 1/2 hours until rice is tender and liquid is absorbed. Serves 6.

1 serving: 298 Calories; 5.9 g Total Fat (1.6 g Mono, 0.8 g Poly, 3.0 g Sat); 66 mg Cholesterol; 40 g Carbohydrate; 3 g Fibre; 22 g Protein; 1130 mg Sodium

Bean And Turkey Bake

Frozen French-style green beans	6 cups	1.5 L
Cooking oil	2 tsp.	10 mL
Lean ground turkey	1 lb.	454 g
Chopped onion	1/2 cup	125 mL
All-purpose flour	2 tsp.	10 mL
Can of condensed cream of mushroom soup	10 oz.	284 mL
Low-sodium soy sauce	1 tsp.	5 mL
Fresh bean sprouts	3 cups	750 mL
Butter (or hard margarine)	2 tbsp.	30 mL
Fine dry bread crumbs	1/2 cup	125 mL

Cook green beans in water in medium saucepan until tender-crisp. Drain. Set aside.

Heat cooking oil in large frying pan on medium-high. Add turkey and onion. Scramble-fry for about 10 minutes until turkey is no longer pink. Drain.

Add flour. Heat and stir for 1 minute.

Add soup and soy sauce. Heat and stir for about 2 minutes until boiling and thickened.

Add green beans and bean sprouts. Stir. Spread in ungreased 2 quart (2 L) shallow baking dish.

Melt butter in small saucepan. Remove from heat. Add bread crumbs. Stir until well mixed. Sprinkle over turkey mixture. Bake, uncovered, in 350°F (175°C) oven for about 30 minutes until golden and heated through. Serves 4.

1 serving: 478 Calories; 24.6 g Total Fat (7.8 g Mono, 6.3 g Poly, 8.2 g Sat); 106 mg Cholesterol; 39 g Carbohydrate; 2 g Fibre; 30 g Protein; 952 mg Sodium

Pictured on page 63.

This one's sure to be gobbled up quickly! Serve with rice or mashed potatoes for a complete meal.

about bean sprouts

Have you ever eaten baby beans? If you've eaten bean sprouts, you have! Bean sprouts are germinated bean seeds that only grow long enough to form shoots. Bean sprouts can be grown from several types of beans but are most commonly derived from mung or soya beans. Sprouts last in the refrigerator for only a few days—so try to use them up shortly after buying. You can also purchase canned bean sprouts but they generally lack the flavour and texture of fresh ones.

One of the easiest to make but so satisfying to eat!

about canned tuna

It's not a fish tale! Tuna packed in water has almost half the calories and only a fraction of the fat that exists in oil-packed tuna. So why even bother with tuna packed in oil? Well, like most things that have a higher fat content, oil-packed tuna has a richer, more flavourful taste. So if you are using tuna to top a salad, you may want to opt for tuna packed in oil. On the other hand, if you are adding flavouring to the tuna, like in a casserole, water-packed will do just fine.

Quick Tuna Casserole

Ingredient	Imperial	Metric
Can of condensed cream of mushroom soup	10 oz.	284 mL
Milk	3/4 cup	175 mL
Salt	1/2 tsp.	2 mL
Pepper	1/4 tsp.	1 mL
Dried oregano (optional)	1/2 tsp.	2 mL
Instant white rice	2 cups	500 mL
Frozen peas and carrots	2 cups	500 mL
Can of flaked tuna, drained	6 1/2 oz.	184 g
Onion flakes	1 tbsp.	15 mL
Butter (or hard margarine)	2 tbsp.	30 mL
Fine dry bread crumbs	1/2 cup	125 mL

Combine first 5 ingredients in large bowl.

Add next 4 ingredients. Stir. Transfer to ungreased 2 quart (2 L) casserole.

Melt butter in small saucepan. Remove from heat. Add bread crumbs. Stir until well mixed. Sprinkle over rice mixture. Bake, uncovered, in 350°F (175°C) oven for about 30 minutes until golden and heated through. Serves 4.

1 serving: 489 Calories; 13.7 g Total Fat (3.4 g Mono, 3.5 g Poly, 5.9 g Sat); 32 mg Cholesterol; 70 g Carbohydrate; 4 g Fibre; 22 g Protein; 1319 mg Sodium

Pictured at right.

Top: Quick Tuna Casserole, above
Bottom: Oriental Tuna Casserole, page 68

Be sure to give this one a try. Water chestnuts add a pleasant, crunchy texture.

Oriental Tuna Casserole

Can of condensed cream of mushroom soup	10 oz.	284 mL
Water	2/3 cup	150 mL
Cans of flaked tuna (6 1/2 oz., 184 g, each), drained	2	2
Cooked spaghetti, cut into pieces (about 2 1/2 oz., 70 g, uncooked)	1 cup	250 mL
Finely chopped celery	1 cup	250 mL
Can of water chestnuts, drained and chopped	8 oz.	227 mL
Unsalted soda cracker crumbs	3/4 cup	175 mL
Finely chopped onion	1/2 cup	125 mL
Finely chopped green pepper	1/4 cup	60 mL
Pepper	1/8 tsp.	0.5 mL
Dry chow mein noodles	1/4 cup	60 mL

Combine soup and water in medium bowl.

Add next 8 ingredients. Stir. Transfer to greased 1 1/2 quart (1.5 L) casserole.

Sprinkle with noodles. Bake, uncovered, in 350°F (175°C) oven for about 45 minutes until heated through. Serves 4.

1 serving: 338 Calories; 9.7 g Total Fat (2.4 g Mono, 4.1 g Poly, 2.3 g Sat); 19 mg Cholesterol; 45 g Carbohydrate; 3 g Fibre; 17 g Protein; 899 mg Sodium

Pictured on page 67.

Surprise Company Dish

White sandwich bread slices, crusts removed	16	16
Cans of flaked tuna (6 1/2 oz., 184 g, each), drained	2	2
Grated medium (or sharp) Cheddar cheese	1 cup	250 mL
Salad dressing (or mayonnaise)	1/4 cup	60 mL
Sweet pickle relish	2 tbsp.	30 mL
Lemon juice	1 tbsp.	15 mL
Prepared mustard	1 tbsp.	15 mL
Seasoned salt	1/4 tsp.	1 mL
Large eggs	8	8
Milk	3 cups	750 mL
Seasoned salt	1/2 tsp.	2 mL
Salt	3/4 tsp.	4 mL
Pepper	1/4 tsp.	1 mL
Cayenne pepper	1/4 tsp.	1 mL

Surprise your guests with tuna sandwiches–casserole style! Remember to assemble this dish the night before.

Line bottom of greased 9 x 13 inch (22 x 33 cm) pan with 8 bread slices.

Combine next 7 ingredients in medium bowl. Spread on bread slices in pan. Cover with remaining bread slices.

Beat remaining 6 ingredients in large bowl until combined. Pour over bread. Chill, covered, for at least 6 hours or overnight. Bake, uncovered, in 350°F (175°C) oven for about 1 hour until golden and knife inserted in centre comes out clean. Serves 8.

1 serving: 396 Calories; 17.9 g Total Fat (6.8 g Mono, 3.0 g Poly, 6.3 g Sat); 255 mg Cholesterol; 30 g Carbohydrate; 1 g Fibre; 27 g Protein; 1047 mg Sodium

The same great taste as a traditional tuna casserole but lower in fat.

about light cheese

Light cheeses often taste a lot more bland than their more fatty counterparts, so consider using a light sharp Cheddar cheese instead of a light medium. It won't be as sharp as regular Cheddar but it will be much more flavourful than other light varieties.

Tuna Casserole

Medium egg noodles	3 cups	750 mL
Cooking oil	2 tsp.	10 mL
Chopped fresh white mushrooms	1/2 cup	125 mL
Diced red pepper	1/2 cup	125 mL
Finely chopped onion	2 tbsp.	30 mL
All-purpose flour	2 tbsp.	30 mL
Skim milk	1 1/4 cups	300 mL
Skim evaporated milk	1 cup	250 mL
Frozen peas	1 cup	250 mL
Can of solid white tuna in water, drained and broken up	6 oz.	170 g
Original no-salt seasoning (such as Mrs. Dash)	1 tsp.	5 mL
Seasoned salt	1/2 tsp.	2 mL
Pepper	1/4 tsp.	1 mL
Whole wheat bread slice, processed into crumbs	1	1
Grated light sharp Cheddar cheese	1/2 cup	125 mL
Chopped fresh dill, for garnish		

Cook noodles in boiling salted water in large uncovered saucepan or Dutch oven for 6 to 8 minutes, stirring occasionally, until tender but firm. Drain. Return to same saucepan. Set aside.

Heat cooking oil in large frying pan on medium. Add next 3 ingredients. Cook for 5 to 10 minutes, stirring occasionally, until vegetables are softened.

Add flour. Heat and stir for 1 minute.

Slowly add both milks, stirring constantly until smooth. Heat and stir for 5 to 10 minutes until boiling and thickened.

Add next 5 ingredients. Stir. Add to noodles. Stir. Transfer to greased 2 quart (2 L) casserole.

(continued on next page)

Combine bread crumbs and cheese in small bowl. Sprinkle over noodle mixture. Bake, covered, in 350°F (175°C) oven for about 30 minutes until heated through.

Garnish with dill. Serves 4.

1 serving: 382 Calories; 8.5 g Total Fat (3.1 g Mono, 1.7 g Poly, 2.9 g Sat); 57 mg Cholesterol; 47 g Carbohydrate; 4 g Fibre; 28 g Protein; 592 mg Sodium

Pictured below.

An extra-special casserole for extra-special people. Treat your nearest and dearest to this fabulous combination.

variation

Not a fan of canned asparagus? Substitute with a can of cut green beans, rinsed and drained. It's just as good!

about red and pink salmon

When used in a casserole, it is hard to distinguish the subtle taste differences between red and pink salmon. The most noticeable difference between the two types is the colour. Red salmon is much more vibrant and will stand out in a casserole, whereas pink salmon may be harder to see.

Salmon Pasta

Large (not jumbo) shell pasta	2 1/2 cups	625 mL
Butter (or hard margarine)	1/4 cup	60 mL
Chopped onion	1/2 cup	125 mL
All-purpose flour	1/4 cup	60 mL
Salt	1/2 tsp.	2 mL
Paprika	1/4 tsp.	1 mL
Dry mustard	1/4 tsp.	1 mL
Milk	3 cups	750 mL
Cans of red (or pink) salmon (7 1/2 oz.,213 g, each), drained, skin and round bones removed	2	2
Can of sliced mushrooms, drained	10 oz.	284 mL
Grated medium Cheddar cheese	1/2 cup	125 mL
Can of sliced black olives, drained	4 1/2 oz.	125 mL
Worcestershire sauce	1 tsp.	5 mL
Can of asparagus tips, drained	12 oz.	341 mL
Butter (or hard margarine)	2 tbsp.	30 mL
Fine dry bread crumbs	1/2 cup	125 mL
Grated medium Cheddar cheese	1/4 cup	60 mL

Cook pasta in boiling salted water in uncovered Dutch oven for 10 to 15 minutes, stirring occasionally, until tender but firm. Drain. Return to same pot. Set aside.

Melt first amount of butter in large saucepan on medium. Add onion. Cook for 5 to 10 minutes, stirring often, until softened.

Add next 4 ingredients. Heat and stir for 1 minute.

Slowly add milk, stirring constantly until smooth. Heat and stir for 5 to 10 minutes until boiling and thickened. Remove from heat.

Add next 5 ingredients. Stir. Add to pasta. Stir. Transfer to ungreased 3 quart (3 L) casserole.

Arrange asparagus on pasta mixture.

(continued on next page)

Melt second amount of butter in small saucepan. Remove from heat. Add bread crumbs and second amount of cheese. Stir until well mixed. Sprinkle over asparagus. Bake, uncovered, in 350°F (175°C) oven for about 30 minutes until golden and heated through. Serves 6.

1 serving: 518 Calories; 24.0 g Total Fat (7.7 g Mono, 2.2 g Poly, 12.7 g Sat); 62 mg Cholesterol; 53 g Carbohydrate; 3 g Fibre; 23 g Protein; 1113 mg Sodium

Pictured below.

Salmon adds interest to scalloped potatoes. A great choice for casual fare. Just add a salad or vegetable, and your dinner is complete.

about Parmesan cheese

Parmesan cheese is a hard, dry cheese made from cow's milk. It has a rich, sharp flavour. A sprinkle of freshly grated Parmesan will improve the flavour of soups, salads, pasta, casseroles and many other dishes.

Considered to be the very best Parmesan cheese, Parmigiano Reggiano is an artisan cheese produced by small farms in Italy's Parma region. The cheese is made by hand using a manufacturing process that has been used for over 700 years. It is aged for two to four years—compared to only fourteen months for American Parmesans. By law, only cheese produced in this way can be sold as Parmigiano Reggiano. To tell whether your cheese is the genuine article, just look for the words Parmigiano Reggiano on the label.

Salmon Potato Scallop

Medium potatoes, peeled and quartered lengthwise	4	4
Butter (or hard margarine)	1/4 cup	60 mL
Chopped onion	1 cup	250 mL
Chopped green pepper	1/4 cup	60 mL
All-purpose flour	1/4 cup	60 mL
Salt	1 tsp.	5 mL
Pepper	1/4 tsp.	1 mL
Milk	2 cups	500 mL
Cans of red (or pink) salmon (7 1/2 oz., 213 g, each), drained, skin and round bones removed	2	2
Butter (or hard margarine)	2 tbsp.	30 mL
Fine dry bread crumbs	1/2 cup	125 mL
Grated Parmesan cheese	3 tbsp.	50 mL

Cook potato in boiling salted water in medium saucepan until tender. Drain. Let stand until cool enough to handle. Slice. Put 1/2 of potato slices into greased 2 quart (2 L) casserole. Set aside.

Melt first amount of butter in medium frying pan on medium. Add onion and green pepper. Cook for 5 to 10 minutes, stirring often, until onion is softened.

Add next 3 ingredients. Heat and stir for 1 minute.

Slowly add milk, stirring constantly until smooth. Heat and stir for 3 to 5 minutes until boiling and thickened. Pour 1/2 of sauce over potato slices in casserole.

Scatter salmon over sauce. Layer with remaining potato slices. Pour remaining sauce over top.

Melt second amount of butter in small saucepan. Remove from heat. Add bread crumbs and Parmesan cheese. Stir until well mixed. Sprinkle over sauce. Bake, uncovered, in 350°F (175°C) oven for about 45 minutes until heated through. Serves 6.

1 serving: 442 Calories; 21.4 g Total Fat (7.2 g Mono, 2.7 g Poly, 10.4 g Sat); 55 mg Cholesterol; 42 g Carbohydrate; 3 g Fibre; 20 g Protein; 988 mg Sodium

Pictured at right.

Top: Salmon Rice Bake, page 77
Bottom: Salmon Potato Scallop, above

Reel them in with this delicately-flavoured seafood shepherd's pie.

about horseradish

Prepared horseradish is made from the root of the horseradish plant, a member of the mustard family. The root has very little of the condiment's characteristic spiciness until it is ground or grated. As it is crushed it releases chemicals that make it hot. The addition of vinegar stops this process, so the hotter the horseradish, the longer the makers have waited before adding the vinegar. Horseradish loses its potency as it ages, so you should buy only as much as you will use in a reasonable amount of time and keep the jar tightly closed in the refrigerator.

Captain's Pie

Medium potatoes, peeled and cut up	4	4
Milk	1/3 cup	75 mL
Onion salt	1/2 tsp.	2 mL
Cooking oil	2 tbsp.	30 mL
Chopped onion	1 cup	250 mL
Grated carrot	1 cup	250 mL
All-purpose flour	3 tbsp.	50 mL
Chicken bouillon powder	1 tsp.	5 mL
Prepared horseradish	1 tsp.	5 mL
Salt	1/2 tsp.	2 mL
Pepper	1/4 tsp.	1 mL
Milk	1 1/2 cups	375 mL
Cod (or other white fish) fillets, any small bones removed, cut into bite-size pieces	1 lb.	454 g
Frozen peas	1 cup	250 mL
Butter (or hard margarine), melted	1 tbsp.	15 mL
Paprika, sprinkle		

Cook potato in boiling salted water in medium saucepan until tender. Drain.

Add first amount of milk and onion salt. Mash. Cover. Set aside.

Heat cooking oil in large frying pan on medium. Add onion. Cook for 5 to 10 minutes, stirring often, until softened.

Add carrot. Cook for 1 to 2 minutes, stirring occasionally, until softened.

Add next 5 ingredients. Stir.

Slowly add second amount of milk, stirring constantly until smooth. Heat and stir for 2 to 3 minutes until boiling and thickened.

Add fish and peas. Stir. Reduce heat to medium-low. Simmer, covered, for about 10 minutes, stirring occasionally, until fish flakes easily when tested with a fork. Spread in ungreased 9 x 9 inch (22 x 22 cm) baking dish. Carefully spread mashed potatoes on fish mixture to edges of baking dish.

(continued on next page)

Brush with butter. Sprinkle with paprika. Bake, uncovered, in 400°F (205°C) oven for about 30 minutes until heated through. Serves 4.

1 serving: 471 Calories; 12.5 g Total Fat (5.5 g Mono, 2.7 g Poly, 3.4 g Sat); 62 mg Cholesterol; 58 g Carbohydrate; 6 g Fibre; 32 g Protein; 825 mg Sodium

Salmon Rice Bake

Water	3 cups	750 mL
Grated carrot, lightly packed	1 1/2 cups	375 mL
Finely chopped onion	1 cup	250 mL
Low-sodium chicken bouillon powder	2 tsp.	10 mL
Small broccoli florets	1 cup	250 mL
Instant white rice	2 1/4 cups	550 mL
Can of condensed cream of mushroom soup	10 oz.	284 mL
Can of red (or pink) salmon, drained, skin and round bones removed	7 1/2 oz.	213 g
Paprika, sprinkle		

Combine first 4 ingredients in large saucepan. Bring to a boil. Boil gently, covered, on medium for 5 minutes.

Add broccoli. Cook, covered, for about 5 minutes until tender-crisp. Do not drain.

Add rice. Stir. Cover. Remove from heat. Let stand for 5 minutes.

Add soup and salmon. Stir. Transfer to greased 2 quart (2 L) casserole.

Sprinkle with paprika. Bake, covered, in 350°F (175°C) oven for about 30 minutes until heated through. Serves 4.

1 serving: 406 Calories; 10.0 g Total Fat (2.6 g Mono, 4.2 g Poly, 2.5 g Sat); 13 mg Cholesterol; 62 g Carbohydrate; 3 g Fibre; 16 g Protein; 1082 mg Sodium

Pictured on page 75.

A colourful combination—you'll make this all-in-one meal often!

food fun

Have you ever heard of a person's skin turning orange from eating too many carrots? It's not a myth. It's a real condition called carotenemia. You have to eat lots and lots of carrots over many successive days to attain such a vibrant hue but, luckily, once you stop eating carrots your skin will regain its natural tone. But this does beg the question: Why aren't all rabbits orange?

Top notch! Colourful vegetables top halibut fillets in this savoury supper.

about parsnips

The parsnip is a root vegetable that resembles a white-to-beige-coloured carrot. The parsnip is favoured for its sweet, nutty flavour. It is a hardy plant that is available year round and can be steamed, boiled, roasted, mashed like potatoes, or thinly sliced and deep-fried into parsnip chips. Buy parsnips with smooth, cream-coloured skin. Avoid limp or shrivelled-looking roots.

Smothered Halibut

Halibut fillets, cut into 4 equal pieces	1 1/4 lbs.	560 g
Butter (or hard margarine)	1 1/2 tsp.	7 mL
Large onion, thinly sliced and separated into rings	1	1
Butter (or hard margarine)	1 1/2 tsp.	7 mL
Medium carrot, grated	1	1
Medium parsnip, grated	1	1
Small zucchini (with peel), thinly sliced lengthwise	1	1
Medium tomatoes, seeded and diced	2	2
Dried basil	3/4 tsp.	4 mL
Salt	1/2 tsp.	2 mL
Pepper	1/4 tsp.	1 mL
Grated Parmesan cheese	2 tbsp.	30 mL

Arrange fish in greased 8 x 8 inch (20 x 20 cm) pan.

Melt first amount of butter in small frying pan on medium. Add onion. Cook for 5 to 10 minutes, stirring often, until softened. Scatter over fish.

Melt second amount of butter in same pan. Add carrot and parsnip. Cook for about 2 minutes, stirring often, until tender. Scatter over onion.

Cook zucchini in same pan for about 2 minutes, stirring often, until softened. Arrange on carrot mixture.

Put tomato into medium bowl. Sprinkle with next 3 ingredients. Toss until coated. Scatter over zucchini.

Sprinkle with Parmesan cheese. Cover with greased foil. Bake in 450°F (230°C) oven for 30 to 35 minutes until fish flakes easily when tested with a fork. Serves 4.

1 serving: 266 Calories; 7.6 g Total Fat (2.3 g Mono, 1.5 g Poly, 3.0 g Sat); 55 mg Cholesterol; 17 g Carbohydrate; 4 g Fibre; 33 g Protein; 331 mg Sodium

Pictured at right.

Thyme changes everything! Serve a salad or steamed vegetables on the side.

homemade bread crumbs

Why spend money buying bread crumbs? You can make your own with the less-than-fresh bread that's probably sitting on your counter right now! Use stale or 2-day-old white or whole wheat bread. Remove the crusts from the bread, if desired. Dry slowly in a 200°F (95°C) oven until dry and crumbly. Cut or break into pieces, then blend or process until fine crumbs form. Freeze bread crumbs in an airtight container or resealable plastic bag.

Fish And Rice Casserole

Water	2 cups	500 mL
Long grain white rice	1 cup	250 mL
Salt	1 tsp.	5 mL
Cooking oil	1 tsp.	5 mL
Chopped onion	1 1/2 cups	375 mL
Ground thyme	1/4 tsp.	1 mL
Halibut (or other white fish) fillets, any small bones removed, cut into 6 equal pieces	1 1/2 lbs.	680 g
Can of tomato sauce	7 1/2 oz.	213 g
Lemon juice	1 tbsp.	15 mL
Granulated sugar	1/2 tsp.	2 mL
Salt	1/4 tsp.	1 mL
Pepper	1/4 tsp.	1 mL
Grated medium Cheddar cheese	1 cup	250 mL
Fine dry bread crumbs	1/4 cup	60 mL

Combine first 3 ingredients in medium saucepan. Bring to a boil. Reduce heat to medium-low. Simmer, covered, for about 15 minutes until rice is tender and water is absorbed.

Heat cooking oil in medium frying pan on medium. Add onion and thyme. Cook for 5 to 10 minutes, stirring often, until onion is softened. Add to rice. Stir. Transfer to ungreased 2 quart (2 L) casserole.

Arrange fish on rice mixture.

Combine next 5 ingredients in small bowl. Pour over top. Spread to sides of casserole.

Combine cheese and bread crumbs in small bowl. Sprinkle over tomato sauce mixture. Bake, uncovered, in 350°F (175°C) oven for about 35 minutes until golden and fish flakes easily when tested with a fork. Serves 6.

1 serving: 506 Calories; 14.6 g Total Fat (4.6 g Mono, 1.9 g Poly, 6.9 g Sat); 68 mg Cholesterol; 55 g Carbohydrate; 3 g Fibre; 37 g Protein; 1377 mg Sodium

Pictured on page 83.

Shrimp Casserole

Fresh asparagus, trimmed of tough ends and cut into 1 inch (2.5 cm) pieces	1 1/2 lbs.	680 g
Large eggs	6	6
Cooked salad shrimp	8 oz.	225 g
Finely chopped green pepper	1/2 cup	125 mL
Finely chopped onion	1/3 cup	75 mL
Salt	1/2 tsp.	2 mL
Pepper	1/4 tsp.	1 mL
Garlic powder	1/4 tsp.	1 mL
Ground thyme, just a pinch		
Grated sharp Cheddar cheese	1 cup	250 mL

Cook asparagus in water in large saucepan until tender-crisp. Drain.

Beat eggs in large bowl until frothy. Add next 7 ingredients. Stir. Add asparagus. Stir. Spread in greased 2 quart (2 L) shallow baking dish. Bake, uncovered, in 350°F (175°C) oven for about 40 minutes until set.

Sprinkle with cheese. Bake for another 4 to 6 minutes until cheese is melted. Serves 6.

1 serving: 222 Calories; 12.3 g Total Fat (3.9 g Mono, 1.1 g Poly, 5.9 g Sat); 310 mg Cholesterol; 7 g Carbohydrate; 2 g Fibre; 22 g Protein; 471 mg Sodium

Who would have thought asparagus and shrimp could be so tasty together? This may be assembled in the morning and refrigerated until ready to bake.

tip

Asparagus can be trimmed in two ways: the ends can be cut off at the point where the asparagus starts to soften and bend or they can be snapped off at this same point. No matter how you trim the ends, consider saving the woody tips for use in making soup stock. Just put the tips in a resealable plastic bag and freeze until needed.

Delicious and attractive. If you prefer a bolder taste, you can substitute the light Cheddar cheese with regular. Use your prettiest casserole dish for a showy presentation.

Seafood Delight

Large eggs	2	2
Mashed potatoes (about 1 1/2 lbs., 680 g, uncooked)	3 cups	750 mL
Grated light sharp Cheddar cheese	1/2 cup	125 mL
Pepper, sprinkle		
Paprika, sprinkle		
Butter (or hard margarine)	2 tbsp.	30 mL
Sliced fresh white mushrooms	1 cup	250 mL
All-purpose flour	1/4 cup	60 mL
Milk	2 cups	500 mL
Dry (or alcohol-free) white wine	2 tbsp.	30 mL
Grated light sharp Cheddar cheese	1 cup	250 mL
Parsley flakes	1/2 tsp.	2 mL
Seasoned salt	1/2 tsp.	2 mL
Pepper, sprinkle		
Imitation crabmeat, cut into bite-size pieces (see Note)	1 1/2 cups	375 mL
Frozen cooked shrimp, (peeled and deveined), thawed	9 oz.	255 g
Frozen tiny peas	1 cup	250 mL
Grated light sharp Cheddar cheese	1 cup	250 mL

Combine first 4 ingredients in medium bowl. Press in bottom and up sides of greased 2 quart (2 L) shallow baking dish.

Sprinkle with paprika. Set aside.

Melt butter in large saucepan on medium. Add mushrooms. Cook for about 5 minutes, stirring occasionally, until softened.

Sprinkle with flour. Heat and stir for 1 minute.

Slowly add milk, stirring constantly until smooth. Add wine. Heat and stir for about 10 minutes until boiling and thickened.

Add next 4 ingredients. Stir until cheese is melted. Remove from heat.

(continued on next page)

Add next 3 ingredients. Stir. Carefully pour into potato shell in baking dish. Bake, uncovered, in 350°F (175°C) oven for about 20 minutes until heated through.

Sprinkle with third amount of cheese. Bake, uncovered, for another 10 minutes until cheese is melted. Serves 6.

1 serving: 480 Calories; 17.7 g Total Fat (5.2 g Mono, 1.2 g Poly, 10.1 g Sat); 199 mg Cholesterol; 42 g Carbohydrate; 4 g Fibre; 35 g Protein; 1000 mg Sodium

Note: Instead of imitation crabmeat, use two 5 oz. (142 g) cans of real crabmeat, drained, cartilage removed, flaked.

Pictured below.

Top: Seafood Delight, page 82
Bottom: Fish And Rice Casserole, page 80

Yum! Soft tortillas stuffed with delectably seasoned seafood are topped with salsa and melted cheese. Garnish with chopped tomato or avocado for a lively twist.

about cilantro

Because cilantro and parsley look similar (and are often mislabelled and put together at the grocery store), people often confuse the two. One sure way of telling them apart is by tasting them. Cilantro has a distinct pungent flavour people either love or hate, whereas parsley is much more mellow tasting. And while parsley is often seen as a plate garnish at the local diner, cilantro is most commonly used in Mexican, Indian and Southeast Asian foods. Dried versions of both cilantro and parsley are available but lack the true flavour of the fresh herbs. If you don't like cilantro, try using fresh parsley instead.

Seafood Enchiladas

Fresh (or frozen, thawed) small bay scallops	1 lb.	454 g
Bag of frozen uncooked medium shrimp (peeled and deveined), thawed	12 oz.	340 g
Water	1 cup	250 mL
Block of cream cheese, softened	8 oz.	250 g
Sour cream	1/2 cup	125 mL
Chopped yellow pepper	2/3 cup	150 mL
Sliced green onion	2/3 cup	150 mL
Can of crabmeat, drained, cartilage removed, flaked	4 1/4 oz.	120 g
Garlic clove, minced (or 1/4 tsp., 1 mL, powder)	1	1
Ground cumin	1/2 tsp.	2 mL
Salt	1/4 tsp.	1 mL
Pepper	1/4 tsp.	1 mL
Chopped fresh cilantro or parsley (optional)	2 tbsp.	30 mL
Flour tortillas (9 inch, 22 cm, diameter)	6	6
Mild salsa	2 cups	500 mL
Grated Monterey Jack cheese	1 cup	250 mL
Grated medium Cheddar cheese	1 cup	250 mL

Combine first 3 ingredients in medium saucepan. Bring to a boil. Reduce heat to medium-low. Simmer, covered, for about 2 minutes until scallops are opaque and shrimp turn pink. Do not overcook. Drain. Chop.

Beat cream cheese and sour cream in large bowl until smooth. Add next 8 ingredients and seafood mixture. Stir.

Spoon seafood mixture along centre of tortillas. Fold sides over filling. Roll up from bottom to enclose. Arrange enchiladas, seam-side down, in greased 9 x 13 inch (22 x 33 cm) baking dish.

Pour salsa over top. Bake, uncovered, in 375°F (190°C) oven for about 20 minutes until heated through.

(continued on next page)

Sprinkle with both cheeses. Bake, uncovered, for another 3 to 5 minutes until cheese is melted. Serves 6.

1 serving: 696 Calories; 36.3 g Total Fat (10.5 g Mono, 3.4 g Poly, 19.9 g Sat); 203 mg Cholesterol; 45 g Carbohydrate; 4 g Fibre; 47 g Protein; 1322 mg Sodium

Pictured below.

food fun

Macaroni and cheese is an all-time favourite comfort food that reminds people of their childhoods. As uncomplicated as the dish seems, its history has been anything but! There has been much feverish debate about who actually invented macaroni and cheese. Some say it was invented in Sicily as early as the 12th century. Some believe that Thomas Jefferson invented it, while others claim that versions of macaroni and cheese were being made in the days of the ancient Romans and Greeks. Imagine that, Socrates and his students discussing life philosophies while supping on mac 'n' cheese!

Macaroni And Cheese

Elbow macaroni	2 cups	500 mL
Butter (or hard margarine)	1/4 cup	60 mL
All-purpose flour	3 tbsp.	50 mL
Onion flakes	1 tbsp.	15 mL
Salt	1/2 tsp.	2 mL
Pepper	1/8 tsp.	0.5 mL
Milk	2 cups	500 mL
Grated medium (or sharp) Cheddar cheese	1 cup	250 mL
Butter (or hard margarine)	2 tbsp.	30 mL
Fine dry bread crumbs	1/2 cup	125 mL
Grated medium (or sharp) Cheddar cheese	1/4 cup	60 mL

Cook macaroni in boiling salted water in large uncovered saucepan or Dutch oven for 8 to 10 minutes, stirring occasionally, until tender but firm. Drain. Transfer to greased 2 quart (2 L) casserole. Set aside.

Melt first amount of butter in same saucepan on medium. Add next 4 ingredients. Heat and stir for 1 minute.

Slowly add milk, stirring constantly until smooth. Heat and stir for about 5 minutes until boiling and thickened. Remove from heat.

Add first amount of cheese. Stir until melted. Add to macaroni. Stir.

Melt second amount of butter in small saucepan. Remove from heat. Add bread crumbs and second amount of cheese. Stir until well mixed. Sprinkle over macaroni mixture. Bake, uncovered, in 350°F (175°C) oven for about 30 minutes until golden. Serves 4.

1 serving: 653 Calories; 33.6 g Total Fat (9.5 g Mono, 1.7 g Poly, 20.3 g Sat); 93 mg Cholesterol; 64 g Carbohydrate; 3 g Fibre; 23 g Protein; 905 mg Sodium

Pictured at right.

Simple to prepare, with out-of-the-ordinary results! Delicious served with bruschetta or a tossed salad.

easy lemon pepper

Lemon pepper is a popular addition to many foods, but did you know that it's easy and inexpensive to make yourself? Follow these simple steps to make a deliciously bold version of this popular seasoning:

1. Remove zest from 1 lemon.
2. Mince zest and transfer to a small bowl.
3. Add 2 tsp. (10 mL) of coarsely cracked peppercorns.
4. Use a sturdy wooden spoon to crush the pepper and zest.
5. Spread the lemon pepper mixture on a baking sheet and bake in a 200°F (95°C) oven until mixture is dry.
6. Grind or mince the mixture finely.

Crunchy Vegetable Macaroni

Water	2 1/2 cups	625 mL
Thinly sliced carrot	1/3 cup	75 mL
Sugar snap peas, trimmed	1 cup	250 mL
Fresh asparagus, trimmed of tough ends and cut into 1 inch (2.5 cm) pieces	7 oz.	200 g
Diced red pepper	1/4 cup	60 mL
Ice water		
Can of skim evaporated milk	13 1/2 oz.	385 mL
Garlic and herb no-salt seasoning (such as Mrs. Dash)	1 tsp.	5 mL
Lemon pepper	1/2 tsp.	2 mL
Whole wheat elbow macaroni	2 cups	500 mL
Grated light sharp Cheddar cheese	1 cup	250 mL
Green onions, thinly sliced	2	2

Chopped fresh parsley, for garnish

Measure water into large saucepan. Bring to a boil. Add carrot. Cook, covered, for 4 minutes.

Add next 3 ingredients. Cook, covered, for 3 minutes. Immediately transfer vegetables with slotted spoon to large bowl of ice water. Let vegetables stand until cool. Reserve 2 cups (500 mL) cooking liquid. Drain. Set aside.

Combine reserved cooking liquid and next 3 ingredients in same saucepan. Bring to a boil.

Add macaroni. Cook, uncovered, for about 15 minutes, stirring often, until macaroni is tender and liquid is almost absorbed. Do not drain.

Add vegetables, cheese and green onion. Stir. Transfer to greased 3 quart (3 L) casserole. Bake, covered, in 350°F (175°C) oven for about 30 minutes until heated through.

Garnish with parsley. Serves 4.

1 serving: 405 Calories; 7.2 g Total Fat (2.0 g Mono, 0.5 g Poly, 4.1 g Sat); 22 mg Cholesterol; 62 g Carbohydrate; 2 g Fibre; 26 g Protein; 405 mg Sodium

Pictured at right.

Same great flavour, without the fuss!
Serve with a dollop of sour cream.

Lazy Perogy Casserole

Lasagna noodles	15	15
Large egg	1	1
2% cottage cheese	2 cups	500 mL
Onion salt	1/4 tsp.	1 mL
Mashed potatoes (about 1 lb., 454 g, uncooked)	2 cups	500 mL
Grated medium Cheddar cheese	1 cup	250 mL
Onion salt	1/4 tsp.	1 mL
Salt	1/4 tsp.	1 mL
Pepper	1/8 tsp.	0.5 mL
Butter (or hard margarine)	1/2 cup	125 mL
Chopped onion	1 cup	250 mL

Cook noodles in boiling salted water in uncovered Dutch oven for 12 to 14 minutes, stirring occasionally, until tender but firm. Drain. Rinse with cold water. Drain. Set aside.

Combine next 3 ingredients in small bowl. Set aside.

Combine next 5 ingredients in medium bowl. Set aside.

Melt butter in medium frying pan. Add onion. Cook on medium for about 10 minutes, stirring often, until very soft. Layer ingredients in greased 9 x 13 inch (22 x 33 cm) pan as follows:

1. 5 lasagna noodles
2. Cottage cheese mixture
3. 5 lasagna noodles
4. Potato mixture
5. 5 lasagna noodles
6. Onion mixture

Cover with greased foil. Bake for 30 to 40 minutes in 350°F (175°C) oven until heated through. Let stand for 10 minutes before serving. Serves 8.

1 serving: 414 Calories; 19.5 g Total Fat (5.6 g Mono, 1.0 g Poly, 11.7 g Sat); 80 mg Cholesterol; 41 g Carbohydrate; 2 g Fibre; 19 g Protein; 623 mg Sodium

Pictured at right.

Several steps in the preparation but truly worth the time! Colourful, creamy and sure to impress.

Vegetarian Pesto Lasagna

Medium eggplants, cut lengthwise into 1/3 inch (1 cm) slices	3	3
Salt	2 tsp.	10 mL
Olive (or cooking) oil	2 1/2 tbsp.	37 mL

PARSLEY BASIL PESTO

Pecan pieces, toasted (see Tip)	1/2 cup	125 mL
Fresh basil leaves, lightly packed	1/2 cup	125 mL
Fresh parsley sprigs, lightly packed	1/2 cup	125 mL
Olive (or cooking) oil	1/3 cup	75 mL
Grated Parmesan cheese	3 tbsp.	50 mL
Garlic cloves, quartered	2	2
Salt	1/4 tsp.	1 mL
Pepper	1/4 tsp.	1 mL

CHEESE SAUCE

Butter (or hard margarine)	1/4 cup	60 mL
All-purpose flour	1/4 cup	60 mL
Milk	2 1/4 cups	550 mL
Grated part-skim mozzarella cheese	1/3 cup	75 mL
Grated Parmesan cheese	1/4 cup	60 mL
Ground nutmeg	1/2 tsp.	2 mL
Pepper, just a pinch		
Tomato pasta sauce	3 cups	750 mL
Oven-ready lasagna noodles	9	9
Jars of roasted red peppers (13 oz., 370 mL, each), drained, blotted dry, cut into 1/2 inch (12 mm) strips	2	2

Sprinkle both sides of eggplant slices with salt. Place on wire racks set on baking sheets with sides. Let stand for 20 minutes. Rinse with cold water. Blot dry with paper towels.

Brush both sides of eggplant slices with olive oil. Arrange on ungreased baking sheets. Bake in 375°F (190°C) oven for 50 to 55 minutes, turning slices over and switching position of baking sheets at halftime, until softened.

(continued on next page)

Parsley Basil Pesto: Process all 8 ingredients in blender or food processor until smooth. Makes about 3/4 cup (175 mL) pesto. Spread on 1 side of eggplant slices. Set aside.

Cheese Sauce: Melt butter in medium saucepan on medium. Add flour. Heat and stir for 1 minute.

Slowly add milk, stirring constantly until smooth. Heat and stir for about 10 minutes until boiling and thickened. Remove from heat.

Add next 4 ingredients. Stir until Parmesan cheese is melted. Set aside. Makes about 2 1/4 cups (550 mL) sauce.

Layer ingredients in greased 9 x 13 inch (22 x 33 cm) pan as follows:

1. 1 cup (250 mL) pasta sauce
2. 3 lasagna noodles
3. 1/2 of eggplant slices
4. 1/2 of red pepper strips
5. 1 cup (250 mL) pasta sauce
6. 3 lasagna noodles
7. 1/2 of eggplant slices
8. 1/2 of red pepper strips
9. 1 cup (250 mL) pasta sauce
10. 3 lasagna noodles
11. Cheese Sauce

Cover with greased foil. Bake in 350°F (175°C) oven for about 1 hour until bubbling at edges and noodles are tender. Remove foil. Broil for 10 to 15 minutes until golden. Let stand for 10 minutes before serving. Serves 8.

1 serving: 563 Calories; 34.0 g Total Fat (18.6 g Mono, 4.4 g Poly, 9.0 g Sat); 27 mg Cholesterol; 55 g Carbohydrate; 8 g Fibre; 14 g Protein; 1491 mg Sodium

Pictured on page 95.

> **tip**
>
> To toast pecans, place them in an ungreased shallow frying pan. Heat on medium for 3 to 5 minutes, stirring often, until golden. To bake, spread them evenly in an ungreased shallow pan. Bake in a 350°F (175°C) oven for 5 to 10 minutes, stirring or shaking often, until golden.

Make lunch time fiesta time! Polenta goes well with Mexican seasonings and tomato. Definitely one to try.

Polenta Lasagna

Chunky salsa	2 cups	500 mL
Package of veggie ground round	12 oz.	340 g
Polenta roll, cut into 24 slices	2 1/4 lbs.	1 kg
Grated jalapeño Monterey Jack cheese	2 cups	500 mL

Combine salsa and ground round in large bowl. Spread 1/3 of salsa mixture in greased 9 x 13 inch (22 x 33 cm) baking dish.

Arrange 12 polenta slices on salsa mixture. Spread another 1/3 of salsa mixture on polenta.

Sprinkle with 1/2 of cheese. Layer with remaining polenta slices, salsa mixture and cheese. Bake, uncovered, in 350°F (175°C) oven for about 45 minutes until cheese is melted and polenta is softened. Serves 6.

1 serving: 368 Calories; 14.3 g Total Fat (4.4 g Mono, 1 g Poly, 7.7 g Sat); 35 mg Cholesterol; 37 g Carbohydrate; 2 g Fibre; 24 g Protein; 725 mg Sodium

Rich tomato flavour complements tender eggplant in this Italian favourite. Serve with a crisp green salad and garlic toast.

Eggplant Parmigiana

Medium eggplants, peeled and cut crosswise into 1/2 inch (12 mm) slices	2	2
Salt, sprinkle		
Salt	1/4 tsp.	1 mL
Pepper	1/4 tsp.	1 mL
Cooking oil, approximately	2 – 3 tbsp.	30 – 50 mL
Can of tomato sauce	14 oz.	398 mL
Fresh oregano leaves (or 1/4 tsp., 1 mL, dried)	1 tsp.	5 mL
Garlic clove, minced (or 1/4 tsp., 1 mL, powder)	1	1
Grated part-skim mozzarella cheese	2 cups	500 mL
Grated Parmesan cheese	1/2 cup	125 mL
Chopped fresh oregano leaves, for garnish		

Sprinkle both sides of eggplant slices with salt. Place on wire racks set on baking sheets with sides. Let stand for 20 minutes. Rinse with cold water. Blot dry with paper towels.

(continued on next page)

Sprinkle eggplant slices with salt and pepper. Heat 1 tbsp. (15 mL) cooking oil in large frying pan on medium-high. Add eggplant slices in several batches. Cook for about 2 minutes per side until browned, adding more cooking oil if necessary to prevent sticking. Transfer to large plate.

Combine next 3 ingredients in small bowl.

Arrange 1/2 of eggplant slices in greased 2 quart (2 L) casserole. Layer with 1/2 of tomato sauce mixture, 1/2 of mozzarella cheese and 1/2 of Parmesan cheese. Repeat with remaining ingredients. Bake, covered, in 350°F (175°C) oven for about 30 minutes until heated through and sauce is bubbling. Bake, uncovered, for another 10 to 15 minutes until cheese is golden. Let stand for 10 minutes.

Garnish with oregano. Serves 6.

1 serving: 247 Calories; 14 g Total Fat (5.4 g Mono, 1.8 g Poly, 6.2 g Sat); 31 mg Cholesterol; 16 g Carbohydrate; 5 g Fibre; 16 g Protein; 875 mg Sodium

Pictured below.

Top: Eggplant Parmigiana, page 94
Bottom: Vegetarian Pesto Lasagna, page 92

Deliciously rich and full of tomato goodness. Whole wheat pasta adds a nutty flavour to this casserole.

about tube pastas

If macaroni is the only tube pasta you can name, it might be time to explore your pastabilities!

If you want to make your casserole more decorative, rebel against the same old, same old, and try a new type of pasta. Whether you are looking at your local supermarket or hitting the specialty stores, check out the pasta selection to see what exciting varieties they have. Here are some pastas you may want to consider:

Calamaretti	Mezzani
Canneroni	Mostaccioli
Cannolicchi	Pasta al ceppo
Cavatappi	Penne rigate
Garganelli	Pennette
Maccheroncelli	Rigatoni
Magliette	Ziti

Eggplant Pasta Bake

Whole wheat penne (or other tube) pasta	2 cups	500 mL
Medium eggplants, peeled and cut lengthwise into 1/4 inch (6 mm) slices	2	2
Salt, sprinkle		
Olive (or cooking) oil	1 tbsp.	15 mL
Chopped onion	1 cup	250 mL
Tomato pasta sauce	2 3/4 cups	675 mL
Roma (plum) tomatoes, chopped	6	6
Basil pesto	1/4 cup	60 mL
Grated Parmesan cheese	1/2 cup	125 mL
Grated part-skim mozzarella cheese	1/2 cup	125 mL

Cook pasta in boiling salted water in large uncovered saucepan or Dutch oven for 8 to 10 minutes, stirring occasionally, until tender but firm. Drain. Return to same saucepan. Set aside.

Sprinkle both sides of eggplant slices with salt. Place on wire rack set on baking sheet with sides. Let stand for 20 minutes. Rinse with cold water. Blot dry with paper towels. Spray both sides of eggplant slices with cooking spray. Preheat gas barbecue to medium (see Note). Cook eggplant on greased grill for 2 to 3 minutes per side until golden. Transfer to large plate. Cut into 1 inch (2.5 cm) pieces. Add to pasta.

Heat olive oil in small frying pan on medium. Add onion. Cook for 5 to 10 minutes, stirring often, until softened. Add to pasta. Stir.

Add next 3 ingredients. Stir. Transfer to greased 3 quart (3 L) casserole.

Sprinkle with both cheeses. Bake, uncovered, in 350°F (175°C) oven for 30 to 40 minutes until heated through and cheese is golden. Serves 6.

1 serving: 447 Calories; 16.6 g Total Fat (8.3 g Mono, 2.6 g Poly, 4.5 g Sat); 13 mg Cholesterol; 64 g Carbohydrate; 7 g Fibre; 17 g Protein; 828 mg Sodium

Pictured at right.

Note: If preferred, cook eggplant slices in 3 batches in 1 tbsp. (15 mL) olive (or cooking) oil in large frying pan on medium for 2 minutes per side until golden.

This meatless shepherd's pie is packed with so many vegetables and lentils—you won't miss the meat at all!

about lentils

Previously branded as humble sustenance for the less-fortunate, lentils have been steadily gaining in popularity due to their high protein content. Lentils are also considered to be the most easily digested protein source, meat or vegetable. The most common varieties are green, red and yellow. If some of your friends or family are vegetarians, they will delight in being served a lentil dish like Vegetable Shepherd's Pie.

Vegetable Shepherd's Pie

Large potatoes, peeled and cut up	4	4
Light sour cream	1/3 cup	75 mL
Cooking oil	2 tsp.	10 mL
Medium carrots, thinly sliced	2	2
Medium onion, diced	1	1
Garlic clove, minced (or 1/4 tsp., 1 mL, powder)	1	1
Medium zucchini (with peel), diced	1	1
Sliced fresh white mushrooms	1 cup	250 mL
Can of diced tomatoes, drained	28 oz.	796 mL
Can of lentils, rinsed and drained	19 oz.	540 mL
Vegetable bouillon cube	1/5 oz.	6 g
Dried basil	1 tsp.	5 mL
Dried oregano	1 tsp.	5 mL
Salt	1/4 tsp.	1 mL
Pepper	1/2 tsp.	2 mL
Grated Parmesan cheese	3 tbsp.	50 mL

Cook potato in boiling salted water in large saucepan until tender. Drain.

Add sour cream. Mash. Cover. Set aside.

Heat cooking oil in large saucepan or Dutch oven on medium-high. Add next 3 ingredients. Cook for 5 minutes, stirring often.

Add zucchini and mushrooms. Cook for another 4 to 5 minutes, stirring often, until carrot is tender-crisp.

Add next 7 ingredients. Stir. Reduce heat to medium-low. Simmer, uncovered, for about 20 minutes, stirring occasionally, until slightly thickened. Transfer to greased 3 quart (3 L) casserole.

Spread mashed potatoes on vegetable mixture. Sprinkle with Parmesan cheese. Bake, uncovered, in 350°F (175°C) oven for 30 to 35 minutes until heated through. Broil for about 5 minutes until cheese is golden. Serves 8.

1 serving: 211 Calories; 3.3 g Total Fat (1.4 g Mono, 0.7 g Poly, 1.6 g Sat); 4 mg Cholesterol; 39 g Carbohydrate; 6 g Fibre; 9 g Protein; 515 mg Sodium

Pictured at right.

Dress up dinner with a medley of colour. Be sure to try the variation.

southwestern casserole

Instead of whole wheat crackers and Edam cheese, use the same amount of crushed unsalted corn chips and grated jalapeño Monterey Jack cheese for a sensational south-of-the-border flavour.

Rice Veggie Casserole

Canned diced tomatoes, drained	1 1/2 cups	375 mL
Chopped onion	1 cup	250 mL
Sliced celery	1 cup	250 mL
Chili powder	2 tsp.	10 mL
Can of red kidney beans, rinsed and drained	14 oz.	398 mL
Chopped green pepper	1 1/2 cups	375 mL
Can of kernel corn, drained	12 oz.	341 mL
Cooked long grain brown rice (about 1/3 cup, 75 mL, uncooked)	1 cup	250 mL
Salt	1/4 tsp.	1 mL
Pepper	1/8 tsp.	0.5 mL
Coarsely crushed whole wheat crackers	1/2 cup	125 mL
Grated Edam cheese	1/2 cup	125 mL

Combine first 4 ingredients in large saucepan. Bring to a boil. Reduce heat to medium-low. Simmer, covered, for 5 minutes, stirring occasionally. Remove from heat.

Add next 6 ingredients. Stir. Transfer to greased 2 quart (2 L) casserole. Bake, covered, in 350°F (175°C) oven for 15 minutes.

Sprinkle with crushed crackers and cheese. Bake, uncovered, for another 10 to 15 minutes until bubbling at edges and cheese is melted. Serves 6.

1 serving: 234 Calories; 5.2 g Total Fat (1.8 g Mono, 0.7 g Poly, 2.1 g Sat); 8 mg Cholesterol; 40 g Carbohydrate; 7 g Fibre; 10 g Protein; 589 mg Sodium

Pictured at right.

This casserole's made the day before and chilled overnight before baking. Pop it in the oven the next morning for an easy breakfast or brunch dish.

tip

If you are out of dry mustard, you can substitute 1 tbsp. (15 mL) of prepared mustard for 1 tsp. (5 mL) of dry.

Cheese Strata

White bread slices, cubed	7	7
Grated medium (or sharp) Cheddar cheese	2 cups	500 mL
Large eggs	4	4
Milk	2 cups	500 mL
Dry mustard	1 tsp.	5 mL
Baking powder	1 tsp.	5 mL
Worcestershire sauce	1 tsp.	5 mL
Salt	1 tsp.	5 mL
Pepper	1/4 tsp.	1 mL

Spread bread cubes in greased 9 x 9 inch (22 x 22 cm) pan. Sprinkle with cheese.

Beat remaining 7 ingredients in medium bowl until combined. Pour over cheese. Chill, covered, for at least 6 hours or overnight. Bake, uncovered, in 350°F (175°C) oven for about 45 minutes until golden, centre is raised, and knife inserted in centre comes out clean. Puffiness will settle almost immediately. Serves 6.

1 serving: 328 Calories; 18.7 g Total Fat (5.9 g Mono, 1.1 g Poly, 10.2 g Sat); 189 mg Cholesterol; 20 g Carbohydrate; 1 g Fibre; 20 g Protein; 956 mg Sodium

Pork And Rice Dish

Cooking oil	2 tsp.	10 mL
Boneless pork shoulder butt steaks (about 1 1/2 lbs., 680 g), trimmed of fat	6	6
Salt, sprinkle		
Pepper, sprinkle		
Cans of stewed tomatoes (14 oz., 398 mL, each), with juice, broken up	2	2
Long grain white rice	1 cup	250 mL
Boiling water	1/2 cup	125 mL
Beef bouillon powder	1 tbsp.	15 mL
Onion flakes	1 tbsp.	15 mL
Granulated sugar	1 tsp.	5 mL
Pepper	1/4 tsp.	1 mL
Butter (or hard margarine)	2 tbsp.	30 mL
Grated medium Cheddar cheese	3/4 cup	175 mL
Fine dry bread crumbs	1/2 cup	125 mL

An appetizing sprinkling of cheesy bread crumbs makes these chops tops!

freezing pork

Pork can be frozen for different periods of time depending on the cut and the preservation process used. Roasts can stay in the freezer for 4 to 8 months, chops for 3 to 4 months and sausage 1 to 2 months. Pork stored longer than this will be edible but the flavour and texture might be compromised. If frozen pork starts to look dry and greyish-brown it's most likely freezer-burned. To avoid this, always remember to wrap well.

Heat cooking oil in large frying pan on medium-high. Add pork. Sprinkle with salt and pepper. Cook for 1 to 2 minutes per side until browned. Remove from heat.

Combine next 7 ingredients in ungreased 9 x 13 inch (22 x 33 cm) pan. Arrange pork on rice mixture. Cover tightly with ungreased foil. Bake in 350°F (175°C) oven for about 1 hour until rice is tender.

Melt butter in small saucepan. Remove from heat. Add cheese and bread crumbs. Stir until well mixed. Sprinkle over top. Bake, uncovered, for another 10 to 15 minutes until golden. Serves 6.

1 serving: 482 Calories; 19.0 g Total Fat (7.2 g Mono, 1.8 g Poly, 8.6 g Sat); 98 mg Cholesterol; 44 g Carbohydrate; 2 g Fibre; 33 g Protein; 956 mg Sodium

Pictured on page 105.

When you're looking for something just a little different, here's one to try. Malt vinegar adds interest to this hearty pork casserole.

food fun

Despite its British-sounding name, Worcestershire sauce is Indian in origin. The recipe was brought to Worcester from Bengal by the English Lord Sandys in 1835. He asked the now-famous chemists John Lea and William Perrins to make up a batch of the sauce he had so enjoyed on his travels. Lea and Perrins found the end result to be completely inedible but, wasting naught, they stashed a barrel of it in the basement. A year or two later they rediscovered the barrel, sampled the contents and found that it had mellowed into a very tasty sauce. In 1838, the partners began to sell the sauce commercially. It was an instant success. The original recipe remains a secret but probably contains vinegar, sugar, soy sauce, tamarind, lime, cloves and anchovies among other ingredients. Even today, Worcestershire sauce is aged in barrels for several years before it is deemed fit for human consumption.

Sweet And Spicy Pork Casserole

All-purpose flour	1/4 cup	60 mL
Granulated sugar	2 tbsp.	30 mL
Boneless pork shoulder butt roast, trimmed of fat and cut into 3/4 inch (2 cm) cubes	4 1/2 lbs.	2 kg
Cooking oil	2 tbsp.	30 mL
Cooking oil	1 tbsp.	15 mL
Thinly sliced onion	2 cups	500 mL
Medium carrots, cut into 1/4 inch (6 mm) slices	3	3
Medium potatoes, peeled and cut into 1/4 inch (6 mm) slices	3	3
Ketchup	1/3 cup	75 mL
Water	1/3 cup	75 mL
Malt vinegar	1/4 cup	60 mL
Worcestershire sauce	3 tbsp.	50 mL

Combine flour and sugar in large resealable freezer bag.

Add pork in 3 batches. Seal bag. Toss until coated.

Heat first amount of cooking oil in large frying pan on medium-high. Add pork in several batches. Cook for about 5 minutes per batch, stirring often, until browned on all sides. Transfer to greased 4 quart (4 L) casserole or medium roasting pan.

Heat second amount of cooking oil in same pan on medium. Add onion. Cook for 5 to 10 minutes, stirring often, until softened. Add to pork.

Add carrot and potato. Stir.

Combine remaining 4 ingredients in small bowl. Add to pork mixture. Stir. Bake, covered, in 350°F (175°C) oven for 2 hours. Stir. Bake, uncovered, for another 20 to 30 minutes until sauce is thickened and pork is tender. Serves 8.

1 serving: 466 Calories; 18.2 g Total Fat (8.8 g Mono, 3.0 g Poly, 4.8 g Sat); 121 mg Cholesterol; 30 g Carbohydrate; 3 g Fibre; 44 g Protein; 345 mg Sodium

Pictured at right.

Top: Sweet And Spicy Pork Casserole, above
Bottom: Pork And Rice Dish, page 103

Convenient and easy, this kid-friendly casserole is one to grow up with!

Wiener Pasta Bake

Cans of condensed tomato soup (10 oz., 284 mL, each)	2	2
Boiling water	2 1/2 cups	625 mL
Chili powder	2 tsp.	10 mL
Elbow macaroni	2 cups	500 mL
Wieners, cut into bite-size pieces	1 lb.	454 g
Sliced fresh white mushrooms	1 1/2 cups	375 mL

Combine soup, boiling water and chili powder in greased 3 quart (3 L) casserole.

Add remaining 3 ingredients. Stir. Bake, covered, in 350°F (175°C) oven for about 1 hour, stirring once at halftime, until macaroni is tender. Serves 8.

1 serving: 325 Calories; 15.0 g Total Fat (6.6 g Mono, 2.0 g Poly, 5.6 g Sat); 28 mg Cholesterol; 35 g Carbohydrate; 2 g Fibre; 12 g Protein; 1099 mg Sodium

Since wieners and beans are usually a hit with kids, why not get them to help with the preparation? Kids just seem to have a magical flair for stirring ingredients! Consider this a casserole enjoyed by kids of all ages.

variation

If you are so inclined, you can always replace regular wieners with tofu wieners to create a vegetarian dish.

Wieners And Beans

Butter (or hard margarine)	1 tsp.	5 mL
Chopped onion	1/2 cup	125 mL
Ketchup	1/4 cup	60 mL
Fancy (mild) molasses	2 tbsp.	30 mL
Brown sugar, packed	2 tbsp.	30 mL
Prepared mustard	1 tsp.	5 mL
Apple cider vinegar	1 tsp.	5 mL
Worcestershire sauce	1 tsp.	5 mL
Dry mustard	1/2 tsp.	2 mL
Wieners, cut into bite-size pieces	1 lb.	454 g
Cans of baked beans in tomato sauce (14 oz., 398 mL, each)	2	2
Can of red kidney beans, rinsed and drained	14 oz.	398 mL

Melt butter in small frying pan on medium. Add onion. Cook for 5 to 10 minutes, stirring often, until softened. Transfer to ungreased 2 quart (2 L) casserole.

Add next 7 ingredients. Stir.

(continued on next page)

Add remaining 3 ingredients. Stir. Bake, covered, in 350°F (175°C) oven for 40 to 50 minutes, stirring once at halftime, until bubbling. Serves 6.

1 serving: 461 Calories; 19.4 g Total Fat (8.6 g Mono, 2.1 g Poly, 7.2 g Sat); 40 mg Cholesterol; 56 g Carbohydrate; 14 g Fibre; 20 g Protein; 1570 mg Sodium

Pictured below.

An oldie but goodie! Common vegetables and inexpensive sausages make a simple, satisfying meal.

variation

Flavoured versions of the basic tomato soup are now readily available on grocers' shelves. To rev up the taste factor in this casserole consider using a tomato soup flavoured with oregano or basil.

Layered Sausage Casserole

Medium potatoes, peeled and thinly sliced	4	4
Medium onions, thinly sliced	2	2
Medium carrots, thinly sliced	4 – 6	4 – 6
Frozen peas	1 cup	250 mL
Pork breakfast sausages (see Note)	1 lb.	454 g
Can of condensed tomato soup	10 oz.	284 mL
Water (1 soup can)	10 oz.	284 mL

Layer 1/2 of potato, 1/2 of onion and 1/2 of carrot in 2 1/2 quart (2.5 L) casserole. Repeat layers with remaining potato, onion and carrot.

Scatter peas over carrot. Arrange sausages on top.

Combine soup and water in small bowl. Pour over sausages, poking with knife in several places to bottom of casserole to allow soup mixture to flow through. Bake, covered, in 350°F (175°C) oven for 1 1/2 hours. Turn sausages over. Bake, uncovered, for another 30 to 45 minutes until vegetables are tender and sausages are fully cooked. Serves 4.

1 serving: 682 Calories; 35.1 g Total Fat (15.6 g Mono, 5.2 g Poly, 12.3 g Sat); 77 mg Cholesterol; 71 g Carbohydrate; 9 g Fibre; 22 g Protein; 1402 mg Sodium

Pictured at right.

Note: Prior to layering the sausages in the casserole, you may wish to poke them in several places with a fork and cook them for 5 minutes in a large saucepan of boiling water to remove some of the fat.

Filled with sausage and cheese—this zippy casserole is especially great for breakfast. May be assembled the night before and baked the following morning. Just make sure to keep it covered in the refrigerator overnight.

food fun

Many casseroles can be called strata. Strata is the plural form of the word stratum—which means a layer in an ordered system. So strata, easily defined in culinary terms, are layers of food compiled to make a, hopefully, delicious dish.

Sausage Strata

White (or brown) bread slices, crusts removed	6	6
Sausage meat	1 1/4 lbs.	560 g
Chopped onion	1 cup	250 mL
Diced green pepper	1 cup	250 mL
Grated sharp Cheddar cheese	1 cup	250 mL
Large eggs	4	4
Can of skim evaporated milk	13 1/2 oz.	385 mL
Prepared mustard	1 tbsp.	15 mL
Seasoned salt	1/2 tsp.	2 mL
Pepper	1/16 tsp.	0.5 mL
White (or brown) bread slices, crusts removed	6	6
Butter (or hard margarine)	1 tbsp.	15 mL
Cornflakes cereal, crushed	1 cup	250 mL

Arrange first amount of bread slices in greased 9 x 9 inch (22 x 22 cm) pan, trimming to fit if necessary.

Scramble-fry sausage meat in large frying pan on medium-high for 5 minutes.

Add onion and green pepper. Scramble-fry for another 4 to 5 minutes until sausage is no longer pink and onion is softened. Drain. Scatter over bread in pan.

Sprinkle with cheese.

Beat next 5 ingredients in small bowl until combined. Dip second amount of bread slices in milk mixture until coated. Arrange on top of cheese. Carefully pour remaining milk mixture over bread. Pan will be very full.

Melt butter in small saucepan. Remove from heat. Add crushed cereal. Stir until well mixed. Sprinkle over top. Bake, uncovered, in 350°F (175°C) oven for about 40 minutes until set. Let stand for 10 minutes before serving. Serves 6.

1 serving: 677 Calories; 38.4 g Total Fat (15.7 g Mono, 4.4 g Poly, 15.7 g Sat); 229 mg Cholesterol; 52 g Carbohydrate; 2 g Fibre; 29 g Protein; 1387 mg Sodium

Pictured at right.

Top: Ham Veggie Scallop, page 112
Bottom: Sausage Strata, above

Great scalloped taste—with meat and vegetables included for a complete meal in one dish!

Ham Veggie Scallop

MUSHROOM CREAM SAUCE

Butter (or hard margarine)	1 tsp.	5 mL
Chopped fresh white mushrooms	1 cup	250 mL
Finely chopped onion	1/4 cup	60 mL
All-purpose flour	1/4 cup	60 mL
Chicken bouillon powder	2 tsp.	10 mL
Paprika	1/2 tsp.	2 mL
Salt	1 tsp.	5 mL
Pepper	1/4 tsp.	1 mL
Milk	2 cups	500 mL
Diced cooked ham	2 cups	500 mL
Medium potatoes, peeled and thinly sliced	4	4
Medium carrots, thinly sliced	4	4
Medium onion, thinly sliced	1	1
Frozen peas	1 1/2 cups	375 mL
Butter (or hard margarine)	2 tbsp.	30 mL
Fine dry bread crumbs	1/2 cup	125 mL
Grated medium Cheddar cheese	1/4 cup	60 mL

Mushroom Cream Sauce: Melt first amount of butter in medium frying pan on medium. Add mushrooms and onion. Cook for 5 to 10 minutes, stirring occasionally, until onion is softened and liquid is evaporated. Remove from heat.

Combine next 5 ingredients in medium saucepan. Slowly add milk, stirring constantly until smooth. Heat and stir on medium for about 10 minutes until boiling and thickened. Add mushroom mixture. Stir. Makes about 2 1/2 cups (625 mL) sauce.

Layer next 4 ingredients, in order given, in greased 3 quart (3 L) casserole. Pour sauce over top, poking with knife in several places to bottom of casserole to allow sauce to flow through. Bake, covered, in 350°F (175°C) oven for about 1 1/2 hours until potato and carrot are tender.

Scatter peas over top.

(continued on next page)

Melt second amount of butter in small saucepan. Remove from heat. Add bread crumbs and cheese. Stir until well mixed. Sprinkle over peas. Bake, uncovered, for another 15 to 20 minutes until golden and peas are heated through. Serves 6.

1 serving: 414 Calories; 12.5 g Total Fat (4.3 g Mono, 1.2 g Poly, 6.1 g Sat); 47 mg Cholesterol; 56 g Carbohydrate; 6 g Fibre; 21 g Protein; 1516 mg Sodium

Pictured on page 111.

Souper Supper

A super casserole—quick 'n' easy!

Can of condensed cream of mushroom soup	10 oz.	284 mL
Instant white rice (1 soup can)	10 oz.	284 mL
Water (1 soup can)	10 oz.	284 mL
Chopped cooked ham	1 1/2 cups	375 mL
Chopped cooked broccoli	1 1/2 cups	375 mL
Processed Cheddar cheese slices, cut up	4	4

Combine soup, rice and water in ungreased 2 quart (2 L) casserole.

Add remaining 3 ingredients. Stir. Bake, covered, in 350°F (175°C) oven for about 30 minutes until rice is tender and liquid is absorbed. Serves 6.

1 serving: 239 Calories; 10.4 g Total Fat (3.2 g Mono, 2.3 g Poly, 4.1 g Sat); 29 mg Cholesterol; 24 g Carbohydrate; 1 g Fibre; 13 g Protein; 1104 mg Sodium

Prepare and serve for dinner tonight, or bake and freeze for a quick heat-and-serve meal. Perfect for a busy day!

design your own casserole

Using your favourite leftovers, and being mindful of the proportions and flavour combinations, combine the following to end up with your own delicious, original casserole:

1. Cooked protein: meat, fish, cheese, beans—in combination or alone.
2. Cooked starch: rice, pasta, potatoes. Use double the amount of your protein.
3. Cooked vegetables: fresh, frozen, canned. Use the same amount as your starch.
4. Sauce: tomato sauce, gravy, canned soup, cheese sauce. Use enough to moisten your ingredients.
5. Seasonings: use your favourites.
6. Topping: cereal, cracker crumbs, cheese, tomatoes, herbs.

Assemble the casserole by mixing or layering everything together, adding the topping last. Bake in a casserole dish at 350°F (175°C) for approximately 30 minutes, until heated through and bubbling.

Ham And Pasta Bake

Elbow macaroni	2 cups	500 mL
All-purpose flour	1/4 cup	60 mL
Onion flakes	1 tbsp.	15 mL
Dry mustard	1/2 tsp.	2 mL
Salt	1 tsp.	5 mL
Pepper	1/8 tsp.	0.5 mL
Milk	2 1/2 cups	625 mL
Chopped cooked broccoli	3 cups	750 mL
Diced cooked ham	2 cups	500 mL
Grated medium (or sharp) Cheddar cheese	3/4 cup	175 mL
Butter (or hard margarine)	2 tbsp.	30 mL
Fine dry bread crumbs	1/2 cup	125 mL

Cook macaroni in boiling salted water in large uncovered saucepan or Dutch oven for 8 to 10 minutes, stirring occasionally, until tender but firm. Drain. Transfer to greased 3 quart (3 L) casserole. Set aside.

Combine next 5 ingredients in same saucepan.

Slowly add milk, stirring constantly until smooth. Heat and stir on medium for 10 to 15 minutes until boiling and thickened. Pour over macaroni.

Add next 3 ingredients. Stir.

Melt butter in small saucepan. Remove from heat. Add bread crumbs. Stir until well mixed. Sprinkle over macaroni mixture. Bake, uncovered, in 350°F (175°C) oven for about 40 minutes until golden and bubbling at edges. Serves 6.

1 serving: 442 Calories; 15.7 g Total Fat (5.2 g Mono, 1.4 g Poly, 7.9 g Sat); 57 mg Cholesterol; 50 g Carbohydrate; 4 g Fibre; 25 g Protein; 1318 mg Sodium

Pictured at right.

Delicious perogies and ham smothered with melted cheese. No need for sour cream—the mushroom sauce does the trick!

Ham Casserole

Bag of frozen cheese perogies	2 1/4 lbs.	1 kg
Can of condensed cream of mushroom soup	10 oz.	284 mL
Water	3/4 cup	175 mL
Cubed cooked ham	2 cups	500 mL
Grated medium Cheddar cheese	2 cups	500 mL

Cook perogies in boiling water in large saucepan or Dutch oven for about 5 minutes until tender. Transfer with slotted spoon to greased 9 x 13 inch (22 x 33 cm) baking dish.

Combine soup and water in small bowl. Pour over perogies. Stir gently until coated.

Scatter ham over top. Cover with greased foil. Bake in 350°F (175°C) oven for about 30 minutes until heated through.

Sprinkle with cheese. Bake, uncovered, for another 12 to 15 minutes until cheese is bubbling. Serves 6.

1 serving: 600 Calories; 27.1 g Total Fat (8.4 g Mono, 3.0 g Poly, 13.0 g Sat); 96 mg Cholesterol; 55 g Carbohydrate; 5 g Fibre; 33 g Protein; 1238 mg Sodium

Pictured at right.

Just the right blend of spices in this stew-like dish. Perfect served on a bed of rice.

beef creole

Not in the mood for lamb? Stewing beef may be substituted for stewing lamb.

Lamb Creole

Stewing lamb, trimmed of fat and cubed	2 lbs.	900 g
Sliced fresh white mushrooms	2 cups	500 mL
Can of diced tomatoes (with juice)	14 oz.	398 mL
Dry (or alcohol-free) red wine	1 cup	250 mL
Sliced onion	1 cup	250 mL
Medium green pepper, slivered	1	1
Bay leaf	1	1
Salt	3/4 tsp.	4 mL
Pepper	1/4 tsp.	1 mL
Dried thyme	1/4 tsp.	1 mL
Garlic powder	1/4 tsp.	1 mL

(continued on next page)

Combine all 11 ingredients in greased 3 quart (3 L) casserole. Bake, covered, in 325°F (160°C) oven for about 3 hours until lamb is tender. Discard bay leaf. Serves 8.

1 serving: *203 Calories; 6.2 g Total Fat (2.4 g Mono, 0.7 g Poly, 2.2 g Sat); 74 mg Cholesterol; 7 g Carbohydrate; 1 g Fibre; 24 g Protein; 383 mg Sodium*

Pictured below.

Top: Lamb Creole, page 116
Bottom: Ham Casserole, page 116

Our recipe for this stew is much quicker to prepare than the traditional version. Smells wonderful and tastes great served with crusty bread.

food fun

Cassoulet is a classic French stew that is made from white beans and any of a variety of meats including sausage, pork, goose, duck and others. Cassoulet is said to have originated out of necessity when French peasants would make a stew out of whatever ingredients they had on hand. The pot used to make the stew was called a cassoul, which gave cassoulet its name.

Cassoulet

Bacon slices, diced	6	6
All-purpose flour	1/2 cup	125 mL
Salt	1 tsp.	5 mL
Pepper	1/2 tsp.	2 mL
Stewing pork, trimmed of fat and cubed	1 1/2 lbs.	680 g
Stewing lamb, trimmed of fat and cubed	1 1/2 lbs.	680 g
Chopped onion	1 1/2 cups	375 mL
Garlic cloves, minced (or 1/2 tsp., 2 mL, powder)	2	2
Dry (or alcohol-free) white wine	1/4 cup	60 mL
Cans of mixed beans (19 oz., 540 mL, each), rinsed and drained	2	2
Can of condensed chicken broth	10 oz.	284 mL
Can of tomato sauce	7 1/2 oz.	213 mL
Ground thyme	1 tsp.	5 mL
Bay leaf	1	1
Smoked ham sausage, cut into 1/2 inch (12 mm) slices	3/4 lb.	340 g
Butter (or hard margarine)	2 tbsp.	30 mL
White bread slices, cubed	3	3

Fresh rosemary, for garnish

Cook bacon in large frying pan on medium until almost crisp. Remove from heat. Transfer with slotted spoon to ungreased 4 quart (4 L) casserole or medium roasting pan. Set aside. Reserve drippings in pan.

Combine next 3 ingredients in large resealable freezer bag.

Add pork and lamb in several batches. Seal bag. Toss until coated. Heat drippings on medium. Add pork and lamb in 3 or 4 batches. Cook for 5 to 10 minutes per batch, turning occasionally, until browned on all sides. Transfer with slotted spoon to casserole. Stir.

Cook onion and garlic in same pan for about 2 minutes, stirring often, until onion starts to soften.

(continued on next page)

Slowly add wine, stirring constantly and scraping any brown bits from bottom of pan. Cook for about 5 minutes, stirring often, until onion is softened. Add to pork mixture.

Add next 5 ingredients. Stir. Bake, covered, in 300°F (150°C) oven for about 2 hours until pork and lamb are tender.

Add sausage. Stir.

Heat butter in large frying pan on medium until bubbling. Add bread cubes. Heat and stir for about 5 minutes until golden. Scatter over sausage mixture. Bake, uncovered, for 1 hour. Discard bay leaf.

Garnish with rosemary. Serves 12.

1 serving: 370 Calories; 14.5 g Total Fat (4.5 g Mono, 1.3 g Poly, 4.3 g Sat); 81 mg Cholesterol; 22 g Carbohydrate; 3 g Fibre; 35 g Protein; 1016 mg Sodium

Pictured below.

Tender eggplant and ground lamb smothered in a creamy sauce. Our version of this traditional Greek dish is lower in fat—so you can enjoy it more often!

greek feast

Want to treat your guests to *Brōma Theōn*? (That's Greek for "food of the gods.") Start the meal with some Greek appetizers such as store-bought spanakopita or hummus served with pita bread. For the main course, serve Moussaka with a Greek salad on the side. Enjoy with a hearty red Greek wine and finish the meal off with baklava for dessert! Add ambiance to your dinner by decorating with a Mediterranean theme and adding some traditional Greek music.

Moussaka

Medium eggplants, cut into 1/2 inch (12 mm) slices	2	2
Olive (or cooking) oil	2 tsp.	10 mL
Chopped onion	2 cups	500 mL
Lean ground lamb	1 1/2 lbs.	680 g
Water	1/2 cup	125 mL
Tomato paste (see Tip)	2 tbsp.	30 mL
Parsley flakes	1 tsp.	5 mL
Salt	1 tsp.	5 mL
Pepper	1/2 tsp.	2 mL
Garlic powder	1/4 tsp.	1 mL
Ground cinnamon	1/4 tsp.	1 mL
All-purpose flour	1/4 cup	60 mL
Salt	1/2 tsp.	2 mL
Pepper	1/4 tsp.	1 mL
Ground nutmeg	1/8 tsp.	0.5 mL
Skim milk	2 cups	500 mL
1% cottage cheese, mashed	1 cup	250 mL
Grated Parmesan cheese	1/2 cup	125 mL

Arrange eggplant slices on greased broiling pan. Broil for about 5 minutes per side until browned. Set aside.

Heat olive oil in large frying pan on medium. Add onion. Cook for 5 to 10 minutes, stirring often, until softened. Transfer to small bowl.

Scramble-fry lamb in same pan for 10 to 15 minutes until no longer pink. Drain.

Add onion and next 7 ingredients. Stir. Remove from heat. Set aside.

Combine next 4 ingredients in medium saucepan. Slowly add milk, stirring constantly until smooth. Heat and stir on medium for about 10 minutes until boiling and thickened. Remove from heat.

Add cottage cheese. Stir.

(continued on next page)

Layer ingredients in greased 9 × 13 inch (22 × 33 cm) pan as follows:

1. 1/2 of eggplant slices
2. 1/2 of lamb mixture
3. 1/3 of Parmesan cheese
4. 1/2 of eggplant slices
5. 1/2 of lamb mixture
6. 1/3 of Parmesan cheese
7. Cottage cheese mixture
8. 1/3 of Parmesan cheese

Bake, uncovered, in 350°F (175°C) oven for 50 to 60 minutes until golden. Serves 8.

1 serving: 317 Calories; 15.5 g Total Fat (6.5 g Mono, 1.1 g Poly, 6.5 g Sat); 64.6 mg Cholesterol; 19 g Carbohydrate; 4 g Fibre; 26 g Protein; 781 mg Sodium

Pictured below.

tip

To store tomato paste when a recipe doesn't call for a whole can, freeze the unopened can for 30 minutes. Open both ends and push the contents through, slicing off only what you need. Then freeze remaining tomato paste in a resealable freezer bag for future use.

Herd your nearest and dearest to the table with our lamb version of shepherd's pie.

serving suggestion

A lovely complement to a lamb dish is peas tossed with butter and liberal sprinkling of fresh mint.

Lamb Shepherd's Pie

Medium potatoes, peeled and cut up	3	3
Butter (or hard margarine)	2 tbsp.	30 mL
Milk	2 tbsp.	30 mL
Cooking oil	1 tbsp.	15 mL
Finely chopped onion	1 cup	250 mL
Finely chopped carrot	1 cup	250 mL
Finely chopped cooked lamb	2 cups	500 mL
Prepared beef (or chicken) broth	1 cup	250 mL
Chopped fresh parsley (or 1 tbsp., 15 mL, flakes)	1/4 cup	60 mL
Tomato paste (see Tip)	3 tbsp.	50 mL
Ketchup	2 tbsp.	30 mL
Worcestershire sauce	2 tsp.	10 mL
Pepper	1/4 tsp.	1 mL
Water	1 tbsp.	15 mL
All-purpose flour	2 tsp.	10 mL

Cook potato in boiling salted water in medium saucepan until tender. Drain.

Add butter and milk. Mash. Cover. Set aside.

Heat cooking oil in large saucepan on medium. Add onion and carrot. Cook for 5 to 10 minutes, stirring often, until onion is softened.

Add next 7 ingredients. Stir.

Combine water and flour in small cup. Add to lamb mixture. Heat and stir for about 2 minutes until boiling and thickened. Transfer to greased 2 quart (2 L) casserole. Spread mashed potatoes on lamb mixture. Score decorative pattern on top with a fork. Bake, uncovered, in 375°F (190°C) oven for about 25 minutes until potatoes are golden. Serves 4.

1 serving: 439 Calories; 18.1 g Total Fat (7.4 g Mono, 2.0 g Poly, 7.0 g Sat); 94 mg Cholesterol; 40 g Carbohydrate; 4 g Fibre; 30 g Protein; 486 mg Sodium

Pictured at right.

Throughout this book measurements are given in Conventional and Metric measure. To compensate for differences between the two measurements due to rounding, a full metric measure is not always used. The cup used is the standard 8 fluid ounce. Temperature is given in degrees Fahrenheit and Celsius. Baking pan measurements are in inches and centimetres as well as quarts and litres. An exact metric conversion is given on this page as well as the working equivalent (Metric Standard Measure).

Pans

Conventional – Inches	Metric – Centimetres
8 × 8 inch	20 × 20 cm
9 × 9 inch	22 × 22 cm
9 × 13 inch	22 × 33 cm
10 × 15 inch	25 × 38 cm
11 × 17 inch	28 × 43 cm
8 × 2 inch round	20 × 5 cm
9 × 2 inch round	22 × 5 cm
10 × 4 1/2 inch tube	25 × 11 cm
8 × 4 × 3 inch loaf	20 × 10 × 7.5 cm
9 × 5 × 3 inch loaf	22 × 12.5 × 7.5 cm

Oven Temperatures

Fahrenheit (°F)	Celsius (°C)	Fahrenheit (°F)	Celsius (°C)
175°	80°	350°	175°
200°	95°	375°	190°
225°	110°	400°	205°
250°	120°	425°	220°
275°	140°	450°	230°
300°	150°	475°	240°
325°	160°	500°	260°

Spoons

Conventional Measure	Metric Exact Conversion Millilitre (mL)	Metric Standard Measure Millilitre (mL)
1/8 teaspoon (tsp.)	0.6 mL	0.5 mL
1/4 teaspoon (tsp.)	1.2 mL	1 mL
1/2 teaspoon (tsp.)	2.4 mL	2 mL
1 teaspoon (tsp.)	4.7 mL	5 mL
2 teaspoons (tsp.)	9.4 mL	10 mL
1 tablespoon (tbsp.)	14.2 mL	15 mL

Cups

1/4 cup (4 tbsp.)	56.8 mL	60 mL
1/3 cup (5 1/3 tbsp.)	75.6 mL	75 mL
1/2 cup (8 tbsp.)	113.7 mL	125 mL
2/3 cup (10 2/3 tbsp.)	151.2 mL	150 mL
3/4 cup (12 tbsp.)	170.5 mL	175 mL
1 cup (16 tbsp.)	227.3 mL	250 mL
4 1/2 cups	1022.9 mL	1000 mL (1 L)

Dry Measurements

Conventional Measure Ounces (oz.)	Metric Exact Conversion Grams (g)	Metric Standard Measure Grams (g)
1 oz.	28.3 g	28 g
2 oz.	56.7 g	57 g
3 oz.	85.0 g	85 g
4 oz.	113.4 g	125 g
5 oz.	141.7 g	140 g
6 oz.	170.1 g	170 g
7 oz.	198.4 g	200 g
8 oz.	226.8 g	250 g
16 oz.	453.6 g	500 g
32 oz.	907.2 g	1000 g (1 kg)

Casseroles

Canada & Britain		United States	
Standard Size Casserole	Exact Metric Measure	Standard Size Casserole	Exact Metric Measure
1 qt. (5 cups)	1.13 L	1 qt. (4 cups)	900 mL
1 1/2 qts. (7 1/2 cups)	1.69 L	1 1/2 qts. (6 cups)	1.35 L
2 qts. (10 cups)	2.25 L	2 qts. (8 cups)	1.8 L
2 1/2 qts. (12 1/2 cups)	2.81 L	2 1/2 qts. (10 cups)	2.25 L
3 qts. (15 cups)	3.38 L	3 qts. (12 cups)	2.7 L
4 qts. (20 cups)	4.5 L	4 qts. (16 cups)	3.6 L
5 qts. (25 cups)	5.63 L	5 qts. (20 cups)	4.5 L

Tip Index

Recipe Index